Helping the retarded:
a systematic behavioural approach

E. A. PERKINS

P. D. TAYLOR

A. C. M. CAPIE

Illustrations: David Baird

First published 1976
Second revised edition 1980
Second impression 1983

© **British Institute of Mental Handicap**
(Registered Charity 264786),
Wolverhampton Road,
Kidderminster, Worcs., DY10 3PP

No part of this publication may be reproduced in any form without prior permission from the publishers, except for the quotation of brief passages for review, teaching or reference purposes, when an appropriate acknowledgement of the source must be given.

ISBN 0 906054 40 0

Printed by
Bewdley Printing Co. Ltd.,
Wribbenhall, Bewdley, Worcs., DY12 1BS

FOREWORD

This book is designed to assist all those concerned with helping the retarded child or adult learn the skills necessary to live as full and useful a life as possible.

We have tried to present the basic rules for teaching new skills and coping with problem behaviour in a simple, systematic manner. Our aim has been to keep technical jargon to a minimum and to illustrate teaching principles with examples of situations which commonly occur when working with the retarded in the home, school, hospital and training centre.

This, the revised second edition of Helping the retarded, *is published in 1980. As a companion to this edition we have written* Teaching basic behavioural principles *which is a manual intended for use by tutors involved in organising courses in behavioural methods of training for staff and/or parents. The manual, also published in 1980, is available from the British Institute of Mental Handicap.*

This work is our joint responsibility and we gratefully acknowledge the valuable assistance given by many colleagues from a wide variety of disciplines, and especially Mrs. M. Allarton for invaluable secretarial assistance.

The Authors

Contents

FOREWORD (iii)

Section I: THE BEHAVIOURAL APPROACH

Introduction 3
Chapter 1 Basic principles of the behavioural approach 5

Section II: TEACHING NEW BEHAVIOUR

Chapter 2 How do people learn? Reinforcers and types of reinforcer 11
Chapter 3 Learning to do the right thing in the right situation 16
Chapter 4 Choosing and using reinforcers for teaching 19
Chapter 5 Ways to teach new skills: prompting, fading and shaping 24
Chapter 6 Ways to teach new skills: chaining 29
Chapter 7 Maintaining behaviour and coping with difficulties 33

Section III: PLANNING TEACHING PROGRAMMES

Chapter 8 Deciding what to teach: new skills; teaching method 39
Developmental Checklist 40
Chapter 9 Keeping records 55

Section IV: COPING WITH PROBLEM BEHAVIOUR

Chapter 10 Causes of problem behaviour and recording problem behaviour 61
Chapter 11 Will punishment work? 66
Chapter 12 First steps in coping with problem behaviour 67
Chapter 13 Extinction 70
Chapter 14 Some methods of extinction: ignoring problem behaviour; time-out; repairing the damage 72
Chapter 15 Rules for coping with problem behaviour 77

Section V: APPENDICES

Appendix A Group work 82
Appendix B Some examples of these principles in action 86
Appendix C Advanced Developmental Checklist 93

Section VI: ANSWERS TO QUIZZES 102

Section I

THE BEHAVIOURAL APPROACH

Introduction

Society has always accepted that people have different skills and abilities and that some children and adults are much slower at learning practically everything than others. The people who are generally slowest at learning have been labelled *mentally handicapped, mentally retarded, subnormal, "of low I.Q."* or *mentally deficient*.

This book is about ways of teaching children and adults who are (usually) labelled in one of these ways. Throughout the book we will talk about the *"retarded"*. We prefer this term because, generally at least, it describes their problem.

If we are looking for an approach which helps retarded people overcome their difficulties, we can begin by asking "What causes the difficulties?" and "What can we do about these difficulties?" In the past, many people have taken their retarded child to the doctor looking for a "cure" but, although the doctor can help the family to cope, the retarded person is rarely "cured" of all his difficulties. We know that retardation is caused by *things that happen to a child* (both before and after birth) by *things that are inherited* or *a mixture* of both of these.

In some cases, a fairly clear idea of where things are wrong has been found, such as Down's Syndrome (mongolism), but in most instances such knowledge is still lacking. Unfortunately, even when a cause is known, this does not tell us how best to help overcome the resultant problems. We believe that research into the *prevention* of retardation must continue and that *specialist assistance* must be made available at an early stage to all the retarded but that the greatest need at present is to *help people caring for the retarded*, e.g. parents, nurses, teachers and adult training centre staff, to do as much for them as possible NOW.

Basically, children and adults are described as "retarded" because they have failed to learn the skills that are necessary to lead independent lives. They may also have learned to do some things—wave their fingers in front of their faces, talk meaninglessly, or sit and rock for hours in a chair—which are not acceptable to other people.

What follows is an attempt to provide a practical introduction to what we consider is the most effective approach to teaching new skills and activities to retarded people. The methods we describe have been shown to work in many different places, with both retarded children and adults. It must be said that to use the approach properly and effectively a great deal of effort is required. We are sure that those who are prepared to make the effort will find it worthwhile from the results they achieve.

If you want to get the most out of this book, don't try and read it through quickly. Instead, take your time, complete the quizzes and exercises and get a partner or colleague to go over them with you.

If you are a parent trying to use these methods, be sure to tell others working with your child—teachers, doctors, nursing staff— what you are doing. This may help them also.

If you are a tutor intending to organise courses in the behavioural approach for groups of parents or staff, and are proposing to use *Helping the retarded* as the basic text, you may be interested in the companion book which is now published—*Teaching basic behavioural principles: a manual for course tutors*. As its title suggests, we have written this manual specifically to aid tutors of such courses. The manual is available from: BIMH Publications, British Institute of Mental Handicap, Wolverhampton Road, Kidderminster, Worcs. DY10 3PP.

Chapter 1

Basic principles of the behavioural approach

We know that retarded people find learning difficult. We also know that they can learn a wide variety of skills if teaching is properly organised. This book describes the behavioural approach to teaching. It has been used to teach washing, dressing, toothbrushing, reading, writing, language and a great many other important skills needed in the home, ward or place of work. The behavioural approach has also been used to cope with problem behaviour like headbanging, temper tantrums, stealing and fighting.

It is based on the following principles:—

1. *Behaviour is anything a person does that can be observed*

Behaviour is an activity—like talking, sitting down, hitting someone, tightening a bolt, putting on a sock, looking at someone, picking up a book and so on. We can all see others doing these things and agree on what they are doing. Hence it is possible to describe behaviour very accurately.

Behaviour is *NOT* something like feeling angry, loving, frustrated or jealous. These are very rough ways of describing someone's behaviour.

Behaviour is NOT something like feeling angry, loving, frustrated or jealous

Example :

"Bill is frustrated" might mean that he runs up and down the ward screaming and hitting people. On the other hand, it could mean that he sits all day in a chair, rocking. It might even mean that he bangs his head or bites himself.

The word "frustrated" is much too vague. It doesn't tell us enough about Bill to be able to help him The same applies to words like "aggressive" or "destructive". They are much too vague and woolly.

We must know what the person *DOES*, i.e. how he *BEHAVES*, if we are to teach him properly.

2. *Behaviour is learned*

A new-born baby cannot ride a bike, sit in a chair, walk or talk to people. All these skills have to be learned. Almost everything we do is learned.

We have learned to go shopping, use public transport, wash up, work the T.V., drive a car, make a friend laugh, carry out our job, and pretty well everything else we do.

What we learn depends on what happens to us during our lives.

3. *Both good and bad behaviour can be learned*

Unfortunately, people don't only learn good behaviour. They may also learn bad behaviour—like stealing, fighting, temper tantrums and so on. Often, some societies call a particular behaviour "good" whilst others call it "bad". For example, in some Arabian countries it is polite to "burp" after a meal and it is quite acceptable to have several wives.

Obviously, what each person learns depends on what happens to that person during his or her life. They may each learn "good" or "bad" behaviour depending upon their experiences.

4. *Everyone can learn new behaviour*

People are born with differing potential. A retarded child is unlikely to become an atomic physicist and a woman is unlikely to become a heavyweight boxing champion.

Retarded people find learning difficult *BUT* we do know that they can learn. Teaching must, however, be carried out systematically.

The rest of this book describes what is known about how people learn and how this information can be used to teach as effectively as possible.

We all learn according to these basic principles but, because the retarded find learning difficult, it is doubly important to apply these principles systematically.

SUMMARY
1. Behaviour is anything a person does that can be observed.
2. Behaviour is learned.
3. Both *good* and *bad* behaviour can be learned.
4. Everyone can learn new behaviour.

QUIZ 1
Basic Principles
Please tick only one answer unless otherwise stated.
1. Behaviour is (a) Inherited
   (b) Learned
   (c) Feelings
   (d) Motives

2. Behaviour is (a) When people are being good
   (b) Thoughts, feelings, motives and so on
   (c) Anything someone does that can be observed
   (d) When people are being bad

3. Which things below are behaviour? *Please tick five.*
   (a) Aggression
   (b) Talking
   (c) Eating
   (d) Sitting
   (e) Frustration
   (f) Crying
   (g) Thinking
   (h) Headbanging

4. Which of the following is a behavioural description of a person?
   (a) John is easily frustrated
   (b) Jane is often depressed
   (c) Sam steals food
   (d) Albert is brain damaged

5. *Turn this sentence into a brief behavioural description of Ted:—*
"Ted is aggressive". (Just describe what Ted *does*. Do not give reasons for the behaviour.)

....

....

....

Tick either "True" or "False" for each of the following:—

6. People can learn both good and bad behaviour   True or False

7. Retarded people find learning easy   True or False

8. Retarded people can't learn at all   True or False

Section II

TEACHING NEW BEHAVIOUR

Chapter 2

How do people learn?
(Reinforcers and types of reinforcers)

REINFORCERS

Usually, when people behave, something happens afterwards. For example:
When you smile at someone, he/she smiles back
When you switch on a fire, the room becomes warm
When you drink water, your thirst is quenched

If people like what happens after they behave in a certain way they will be more likely to behave that way in the future.

Example:
Suzie is learning to talk. When she says "Mama" her mother hugs her. Suzie likes being hugged by her mother so she will be more likely to say "Mama" in the future.

The thing that happens after behaviour, which makes that behaviour more likely to recur in the future, is called a *REINFORCER*.

A REINFORCER IS ANYTHING THAT STRENGTHENS THE BEHAVIOUR IT FOLLOWS

Reinforcers strengthen behaviour by making it more likely to happen in the future.

Reinforcers make behaviour more likely to happen in the future

Many different things can be reinforcers and people do not need to be aware of reinforcers for them to work. *Everybody* learns because his/her behaviour has been followed by reinforcers. For example:
You have learned that when you work, you get paid
You have learned that when you ask for a pint of beer in a pub, you will get one
You learned in school that when you worked well, the teacher praised you

Many different things can be reinforcers

A lot of learning is accidental and bad behaviour can be learned as easily as good behaviour.
Example :
Jimmy has a temper tantrum and so his mother gives him a sweet to quieten him down. Jimmy likes sweets, so he will be more likely to have tantrums in the future.

Since reinforcers strengthen behaviour, when we want to teach behaviour we must follow it with a reinforcer.

Getting away from an unpleasant situation can be a reinforcer.
Examples:
Mr. Jones does the washing-up to get away from his wife's nagging.
Mrs. Jones uses tongs to put coal on the fire to get away from burning her hands.
Jimmy's mother gives him a sweet to get away from his screaming.

Getting away from something unpleasant strengthens behaviour like any other reinforcer. However, it is important *never* to use unpleasant events (threats, nagging, etc.) when teaching.

SUMMARY
1. A reinforcer is anything that strengthens the behaviour it follows.
2. People learn to behave because what they do is followed by reinforcers.
3. Getting away from something unpleasant should *never* be used as a reinforcer when teaching.

TYPES OF REINFORCER
We have seen that reinforcers strengthen the behaviour they follow. Many different things can be reinforcers. Different people find different things reinforcing at different times.

Examples:
A baby will probably not find money reinforcing, but may well respond to food.
An adult may not be interested in toys, but will probably find money reinforcing.
We all like different food, music, people and so on.
We are unlikely to find food reinforcing after a heavy meal, but probably would when hungry.

There is a wide variety of reinforcers.

1. **Social reinforcers**
   Things that come from other people, like a smile, praise, attention, a hug, laughter and so on, can act as reinforcers.
2. **Activity reinforcers**
   Doing things like watching T.V., listening to records, playing with a favourite toy, going for a bicycle ride, and so on, can act as reinforcers.
3. **Food and drink reinforcers**
   Items like coffee, sweets, orange squash, crisps, biscuits, ice cream, and so on, can act as reinforcers.
4. **Token reinforcers**
   Token reinforcers are a special type of reinforcer. Tokens can be exchanged for other reinforcers. On their own, they are useless.

Examples:
Money is a token reinforcer because it can be exchanged for a wide variety of other reinforcers, like food, clothing, drink, cigarettes and so on.
Green Shield stamps, luncheon vouchers and cigarette coupons are also token reinforcers.

Anything that can be exchanged for other reinforcers is a *token reinforcer*.

How did all these different events become reinforcing? Some—like food, drink, sex and physical contact—are naturally reinforcing. Other things become reinforcing because they have been regularly followed by the kind of reinforcers listed above. In other words, many reinforcers are *learned*.

Examples:
1. Normally money is not reinforcing for a baby. It becomes reinforcing when the person *learns* that it can be exchanged for other reinforcers, like food, drink, cigarettes, clothes and so on.
2. When a baby says its first word, its mother may say "Good boy" and hug the baby. By being repeatedly associated with hugs, the phrase "Good boy" eventually becomes reinforcing.

Retarded people often haven't learned the value of social and token reinforcers and hence have to be *taught* their value.

QUIZ 2
Reinforcers

Please tick only one answer unless otherwise stated.
1. People learn to do things because:
    (a) They are clever
    (b) They are reinforced
    (c) They work hard
    (d) Learning is automatic

2. A reinforcer is:
    (a) A sweet
    (b) Only used by psychologists
    (c) An event that strengthens behaviour
    (d) A threat

3. A reinforcer:
    (a) Strengthens the behaviour it comes before
    (b) Weakens the behaviour it come before
    (c) Strengthens the behaviour it follows
    (d) Weakens the behaviour it follows

4. If behaviour is reinforced it is:
    (a) More likely to happen in the future
    (b) Less likely to happen in the future
    (c) Slowed down
    (d) Stopped

5. Jane regularly has temper tantrums. She does so because:
    (a) She inherited a bad temper
    (b) She has red hair
    (c) She's bad tempered
    (d) Her tantrums have been reinforced

Types of reinforcer

1. List ten reinforcers that strengthen *your* behaviour.

   (a) ....   (f) ....
   (b) ....   (g) ....
   (c) ....   (h) ....
   (d) ....   (i) ....
   (e) ....   (j) ....

2. Look at the list below and decide what sort of reinforcer each item is. Put **F** for food and drink, **S** for social, **T** for token and **A** for activity reinforcer.

   (a) A box of chocolates   ....
   (b) Green Shield stamps   ....
   (c) A go on the swings   ....
   (d) Being winked at   ....
   (e) Friday's pay packet   ....
   (f) Someone says "Well done"   ....
   (g) A pint of Guinness   ....
   (h) A ride on a bike   ....
   (i) Lunch   ....
   (j) A smile from someone you like   ....
   (k) Reading a comic   ....

3. Can you think of two more *social* reinforcers?

   (a) ....
   (b) ....

4. Can you think of two more *food and drink* reinforcers?

   (a) ....
   (b) ....

5. Can you think of two more *token* reinforcers?

   (a) ....
   (b) ....

6. Can you think of two more *activity* reinforcers?

   (a) ....
   (b) ....

Chapter 3

Learning to do the right thing in the right situation

We have discussed the fact that people learn because their behaviour is followed by reinforcers.

People also learn to behave differently in different places and at different times.

Examples:
    Children learn to urinate in the toilet, not on the floor.
    Children learn to get undressed at bedtime, not in the middle of the day.
    People learn that they can buy groceries from a supermarket, not a drapers.
    People learn that some people will talk to them when they say "Hello", and others will not.

These are very important things to learn. People learn them because they receive reinforcers in some situations but not in others.

Examples:
    You learn that you can buy a drink in a pub in opening hours, but not at any other time.
    Children learn that when they sit at the table at mealtimes they will get food, but they usually will not at other times.
    A child learns that when he talks to his mother she talks back to him, but that nothing happens if he talks when she is not there.

It helps to think of these situations in terms of *green lights* and *red lights*. A green light means you will receive a reinforcer if you behave in a certain way. A red light means you will not receive a reinforcer if you behave in that way. So:—

    The pub opening hours are a *green light* for buying a drink *(reinforcer—drink)*. The pub at any other time is a *red light* for buying a drink *(no reinforcer)*.

    The table at mealtimes is a *green light* for sitting down *(reinforcer —food)*. The table at any other time or anywhere else at mealtimes is a *red light* for sitting down *(no reinforcer)*.

    The presence of mother is a *green light* for talking *(reinforcer— mother talking back)*. The absence of mother is a *red light* for talking *(no reinforcer)*.

People learn that they will receive reinforcers in some situations, but not in others

Green lights and red lights also apply to "bad" behaviour.

Examples:
Johnny urinates on the floor. When he does people rush over to him and he finds this reinforcing. He does not urinate on the toilet.
The floor is a *green light* for urinating.
The toilet is a *red light* for urinating.

When there is one member of staff on duty, all the children play up.
When the ward is fully staffed, they behave well.
One member of staff present is a *green light* for playing up.
All the staff present is a *red light* for playing up.

Green lights and red lights are very important in teaching. People need to know when and where they will receive reinforcers if they behave appropriately.

You can achieve this by making sure people only receive reinforcers for what they do if they do it *at the right time in the right place.*

Examples:
Urinating in the toilet only.
Sitting down at the table for meals at mealtimes.
Getting dressed and undressed at the right time in the bedroom.
Putting on a coat to go outside when it's cold.

SUMMARY
1. **People learn to behave differently in different places and at different times.**
2. **They learn this because they receive reinforcers in some situations and not others.**

3. A green light situation means you will receive a reinforcer for behaving in a certain way.
   A red light situation means you will not receive a reinforcer for behaving in that way.
4. You can teach people the difference between green light and red light situations by only reinforcing them in green light situations.

QUIZ 3
The right thing in the right situation

Please tick only one answer.

1. People behave differently in different situations because:
   (a) They want to
   (b) They have to
   (c) The situation causes them to
   (d) They have learned to

2. James bangs his head when he is taken to the bathroom because he doesn't like baths. This means he usually gets out of having baths.
   (a) What is the green light for Johnny's head-banging? ....

   (b) What is his reinforcer? ....

3. When Freda's father comes home from work, he always brings her a packet of sweets. At six o'clock Freda can always be found waiting by the front door.
   (a) What is the green light for Freda's waiting by the front door? ....

   (b) What is her reinforcer? ....

4. A green light means ....

5. A red light means ....

6. What might be a green light in the following situations?
   (a) Performing on the toilet ....
   (b) Getting dressed in the morning ....
   (c) Buying cakes ....
   (d) Turning on the T.V. ....

Chapter 4
Choosing and using reinforcers for teaching
CHOOSING REINFORCERS

We have seen that there are many different reinforcers and that different people find different things reinforcing. It is important, when teaching someone, to select something that is actually reinforcing for that person. *You can't assume that anything will automatically be a reinforcer; you have to try it out in real life.* It's only a reinforcer if it strengthens the behaviour it follows.

The best way is to actually try out different things which you think might act as reinforcers and see if the person will work for them. To help narrow down the field a little, see what the individual does in his spare time or what he chooses from a variety of reinforcers which you have offered to him.

Let the person choose from a variety of reinforcers

Social reinforcers should always be used with food and drink, activity, or token reinforcers. That way, the value of social reinforcers will gradually be learned and, eventually, you will not have to use other types at all. Many retarded people do not respond to social reinforcers and it is important to teach them to do so. If you *always* use social reinforcers with other reinforcers they *will* learn.

It is often necessary to use a variety of reinforcers as people often become bored if the same toy, activity, type of sweet, etc., is given to them repeatedly. If what you are using stops strengthening the behaviour, it is *no longer a reinforcer*, so try something else.

USING REINFORCERS

We have seen that reinforcers strengthen the behaviour they follow. Hence, the reinforcer should be given immediately after the behaviour you want to teach. There should be *NO DELAY* between the good behaviour and the reinforcer. If there is delay, the wrong behaviour may be taught by mistake.

There should be no delay between the behaviour and the reinforcer

Examples :

Clare puts on her clothes, sits on the bed and begins to rock. Her mother notices that she is dressed and says, "Good girl, now you can go and play". Rocking has been reinforced by mistake and is more likely to happen in the future.

Clare's mother should have reinforced her *immediately* she finished dressing.

Jock is learning to sort items into different containers. He finishes sorting one batch and is sitting doing nothing when the supervisor notices he has finished. She praises him for finishing the job. She has reinforced sitting doing nothing by mistake so Jock is more likely to sit around doing nothing in the future.

Jock should have been reinforced *immediately* he finished the sorting job.

Judy has buttered the bread for the ward tea, but there is no one in the kitchen to see. Judy goes into the corridor and grabs a nurse, shouting "bread, bread". The nurse says, "Good girl, I know you've done the bread" and gives her a sweet. She has reinforced Judy for grabbing and shouting by mistake, and she is therefore more likely to grab and shout in the future.

Judy should have been reinforced *immediately* she finished the bread and butter. (Of course, the nurse could have taught Judy to

come and tell her politely that she had done the bread and butter.)
The other important rule for effective teaching is that, to start with, the behaviour being taught should be reinforced *every time it happens*. The more consistently behaviour is reinforced the better it will be learned.

Since social reinforcers are always available, behaviour can be reinforced every time it happens, even if food and drink, token or activity reinforcers aren't handy.

Let's look at how reinforcers can be used to strengthen desirable behaviour:—

Examples:

The staff on a ward want to encourage the residents to return their plates and cutlery to the serving hatch when they have finished their meal.

Every time they see someone do this they immediately praise him warmly and let him go and sit down in a comfortable chair in the day room.

Trainers in an adult training centre want to encourage their trainees to sit down and work. Hence, every time a trainer sees someone sitting and working she immediately praises him warmly.

She may say things like "Good boy, you are working hard" or "That's good. You're going to earn a lot of money this week".

Mr. Johnson wants his daughter, Lyn, to put her clothes on a chair before going to bed. Lyn does this sometimes, generally after being reminded, but usually leaves her clothes on the floor.

Every time Lyn puts her clothes on the chair, without being told, her father praises her warmly and reads her a special "bed-time story."

Lyn does *not* earn praise or a story if she needs reminding to put her clothes on the chair or if she leaves her clothes on the floor.

Social reinforcers should always be used

Notice that, in each of these examples the emphasis is on reinforcing good behaviour, *NOT* on shouting or telling off the people when they are not doing things right.

SUMMARY
1. Select your reinforcers carefully.
2. Use a variety of reinforcers to ensure that they do not lose their effectiveness.
3. The behaviour should be reinforced *immediately* after it happens.
4. To start with the behaviour should be reinforced *every time* it happens.
5. Social reinforcers can and should *always* be used.

QUIZ 4
Choosing reinforcers
Please tick only one answer unless otherwise stated.

1. All people work for the same reinforcer   True or False
2. If a reinforcer works to begin with it will
   always do so   True or False
3. The best way to choose reinforcers is:
    (a) Pick one you think the person will like
    (b) Use one thing the person chooses from a selection
    (c) Think of what you like and use that
    (d) Use a number of things the person chooses from a selection
4. One reinforcer you always use (though you often use others as well) is:
    (a) A token reinforcer
    (b) A social reinforcer
    (c) An activity reinforcer
    (d) A food and drink reinforcer
5. A reinforcer everyone will work for is:
    (a) A sweet
    (b) Praise
    (c) No one thing
    (d) Food
6. You are going to try to teach a child a new task. How would you go about finding reinforcers you could use with him?
   ....
   ....
   ....

Using reinforcers

Please tick only one answer unless otherwise stated.

1. Reinforcers are best given:
    (a) Immediately before the behaviour you want to teach
    (b) Immediately after the behaviour you want to teach
    (c) As soon as you get round to it
    (d) Any time as long as it's after the behaviour

2. The wrong behaviour may be taught by mistake if:
    (a) The reinforcer is too weak
    (b) The person does not like the reinforcer
    (c) There is a delay in giving the reinforcer
    (d) You're teaching a naughty child

3. We are trying to teach Billy to put on his shirt:—
    Billy puts on his shirt, starts to bite his hands and is then reinforced for putting on his shirt.
    He bites his hands more often because:—
    (a) He's frustrated
    (b) The reinforcer is too weak
    (c) He's trying to attract attention
    (d) He's been reinforced for biting his hands

4. At the beginning of teaching, reinforcers should be given:
    (a) When you're not too busy
    (b) Every other time the behaviour happens
    (c) Sometimes
    (d) Every time the behaviour happens

5. If you haven't got a food or drink, activity or token reinforcer handy you should:
    (a) Ignore the behaviour
    (b) Use a social reinforcer
    (c) Reinforce the behaviour later
    (d) Observe the behaviour

6. Behaviour should be reinforced immediately it happens   True or False

7. To begin with, behaviour should be reinforced only occasionally   True or False

8. Social reinforcers should always be used, even with other types   True or False

23

Chapter 5

Ways to teach new skills: Prompting, Fading and Shaping

PROMPTING AND FADING

We have seen how you can make behaviour happen more often—you reinforce it.

What about when you want to teach someone something new? It's natural to *help* someone who is finding learning difficult. There are three basic ways in which you can help someone to do something:—

1. You can help someone by giving instructions. For example, you can say "Put it in here", "Left hand down a bit", "Tuck your shirt in", and so on.
    This is called a *VERBAL PROMPT*.

Verbal prompt

2. You can help someone by using gestures. For example, you can beckon someone or point at something. This is called a *GESTURAL PROMPT*.

Gestural prompt

Physical prompt

3. You can help people by physically guiding their movements. This is called a *PHYSICAL PROMPT*.

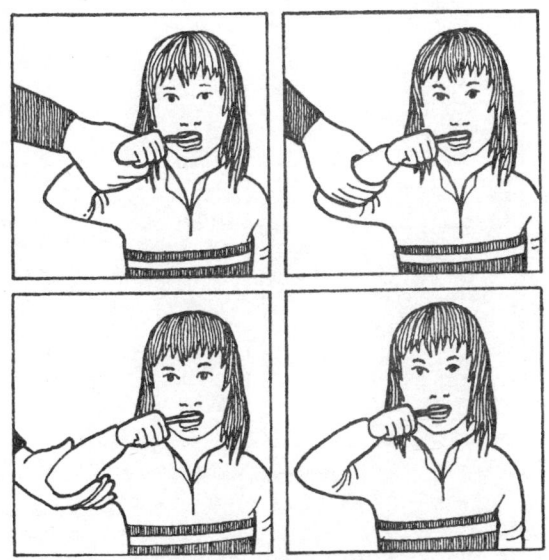

PROMPTS are ways of helping people.

A good way to teach people is to use these prompts to begin with and then *VERY GRADUALLY FADE THEM OUT*. Of course, if you don't fade the prompts out, the person will never learn to do the task on his own. Therefore, you should gradually give less and less help.

Fade out prompts gradually

Prompts are often used as part of other teaching techniques, like *SHAPING* and *CHAINING*. The technique of Shaping is described next. Chaining is described in Chapter 6.

SHAPING

Shaping is a way to help people learn new tasks. You start off by reinforcing behaviour which is only very roughly like the behaviour

25

you are trying to teach and very gradually build up the required behaviour.

Examples:
Jill does not look people in the eye. Her father wants to teach her to look him in the eye when he calls her name. He sits her down and calls her name. He waits until she looks roughly in his direction and then reinforces her. When she does this consistently, he requires her to look at his face before he reinforces her. Gradually over time, he requires her to look at a spot nearer and nearer his eyes before he reinforces her. Eventually, he only reinforces her for looking into his eyes when he calls her name.

Shaping eye-contact

Colin is learning to sort out faulty screws. To start with his trainer deliberately mixes some very distorted screws with some good ones. Colin is reinforced for spotting these and putting them to one side. Gradually, the trainer puts in screws which are less and less obviously distorted, with the good ones, until Colin can sort out screws which are only slightly faulty.

Juliet has not learned to kick a ball. To begin with the nurse reinforces her for simply approaching the ball. Gradually, Juliet is required to stand nearer and nearer the ball to earn her reinforcer. She is then required to touch it with her foot before getting a reinforcer. Gradually she is expected to push it harder and harder with her foot until, eventually, she is kicking the ball before being reinforced.

Using prompts may speed up the shaping process.

Example:
Celia is learning to obey the instruction, "Give me the book". To begin with, father finds Celia will only obey this instruction if it's used with a gesture (holding out hand). So Celia's father begins by holding his hand right out in an obvious way, saying "Celia, give me the book" and reinforcing her when she does so. He withdraws his hand little by little until Celia gives him the book without a gesture.

Claud is learning to sit down when told. His teacher says "Sit down Claud" and, putting his hand on Claud's shoulder, seats him in the chair. The teacher uses this physical prompt to make sure Claud carries out the task properly. Gradually he fades out the prompt until Claud is sitting down without help whenever the teacher says "Sit down Claud".

SUMMARY — To SHAPE new behaviour:
1. Reinforce a behaviour which is very roughly like the behaviour you want to teach.
2. Reinforce the person for behaviour that is gradually more and more like the behaviour you want.
3. Often prompts may help a person learn but they should gradually be faded out.

QUIZ 5
Prompting, fading and shaping

Please tick only one answer unless otherwise indicated.

1. When teaching a new task it is sometimes useful to help the person complete the task properly. This is called:
   (a) Caring
   (b) Prompting
   (c) Abetting
   (d) Modelling
2. What are the three main types of prompts?
   (a) ....
   (b) ....
   (c) ....
3. When teaching with prompts you:
   (a) Keep on using the prompts
   (b) Stop using the prompts suddenly
   (c) Sometimes use prompts and sometimes don't
   (d) Gradually fade out the prompts

4. When teaching a new task you:
   (a) Wait for it to occur and then reinforce it
   (b) Start by reinforcing behaviour only roughly like the one you want to end up with and reinforce gradual improvement
   (c) Get the child to copy you
   (d) Repeatedly tell the child what to do

5. Building up behaviour like this is called:
   (a) Bribery
   (b) Shaping
   (c) Training
   (d) Teaching

6. How would you, using shaping (and prompting if necessary) teach Pete to push a toy car? (You can assume that Pete will sit quietly for reasonable periods, at a table.)

7. How would you, using shaping (and prompting if necessary) teach Jock to thread very small beads onto cotton? (You can assume that Jock will sit quietly for reasonable periods, at a table.)

8. How would you, using shaping, teach a group of six patients, who spend a lot of time rushing about, to sit down for reasonable lengths of time so that you can start teaching them other skills?

Chapter 6
Ways to teach new skills: Chaining

Chaining is another way of teaching new skills.

Many complex tasks are easier to learn if they are broken down into SMALL and SIMPLE steps. The LAST step in the sequence is taught first. When it is well learned the next step is added to it. Gradually more steps are added until the entire sequence has been learned.

This way of teaching is called BACKWARD CHAINING.

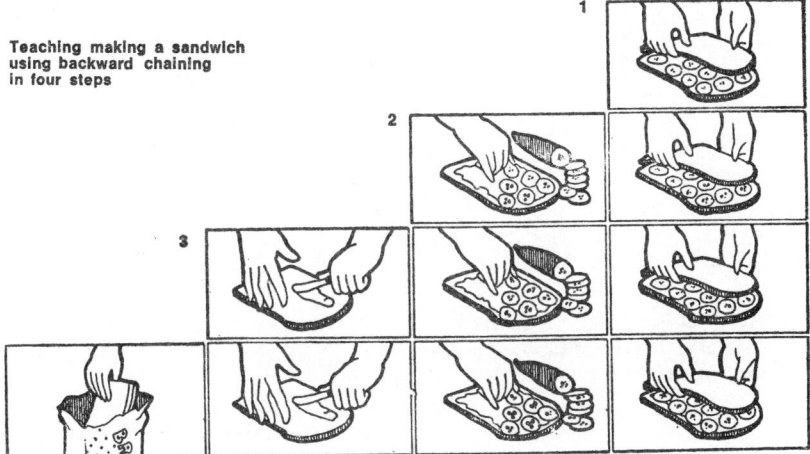

Teaching making a sandwich using backward chaining in four steps

We start by teaching the last step of the sequence so that the person completes the task successfully and is reinforced for doing so. Let us look at some examples of backward chaining in use.

Examples:
Janet's Dad wants to teach her to eat with a spoon. This complex task can be broken down into the following small, simple steps:—
1. Grasp spoon
2. Scoop food onto spoon
3. Lift spoon to within 6" of mouth
4. Lift spoon to within 3" of mouth
5. Lift spoon to within 1" of mouth
6. Put spoon in mouth

To begin with, Janet's Dad puts the spoon in her hand, puts his hand over hers, scoops food onto the spoon, lifts the spoon to Janet's mouth and puts in the food. Notice that he is using a *physical prompt* to help Janet learn.

29

Eating with a spoon broken down into simple steps (of course, these would be taught in reverse order)

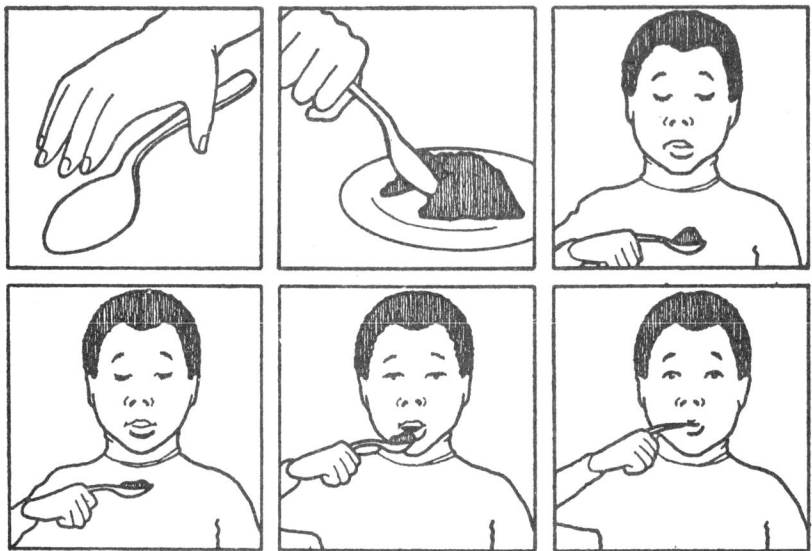

The *LAST* step of the sequence is taught first so, after a while, Dad takes his hand off Janet's just as the spoon is touching her lips. Janet will probably move the spoon the rest of the way, putting it in her mouth.

When she will do this every time, Dad takes his hand off the spoon when it is one inch from her mouth. Janet will probably move the spoon that inch and put the food in her mouth.

When this step is learned Dad will remove his hand when the spoon is three inches from Janet's mouth, requiring her to move it the rest of the way. Gradually the steps are linked up or *CHAINED* until the entire sequence is learnt.

Notice that the reinforcer (in this case the food) is only given after the *last* step of the sequence.

Also notice how Dad gradually *FADED OUT* the *PHYSICAL PROMPT* until Janet was doing the whole task on her own.

John does not obey simple commands. His mother and father want to teach him to obey the command, "John, come here". Having decided that five paces is a reasonable distance to expect John to come, they break the task down into *small* steps.

1. John takes first pace
2. John takes second pace
3. John takes third pace
4. John takes fourth pace
5. John takes fifth pace

They begin by teaching the *LAST* step first.

30

John is stood one pace from his mother who says, "John, come here". As she does so, his father pushes John so that he moves the one pace to mother. He is immediately reinforced. Gradually the father reduces the amount of pushing he does until John has learned to walk the one pace on his own. Notice that John's father is using a *physical prompt* (a push) and gradually *fading it out*. John is then moved two paces away and, when his mother calls, "John, come here", his father pushes him towards mother who reinforces him.

Once again the amount of help the father gives is gradually reduced until John will take two steps to his mother, without help, when he hears her say, "John, come here". Gradually, working backwards through the sequence, more steps are added until the whole task is learned thoroughly.

Bert is being taught how to pack three glasses in a cardboard box. This task can be broken down into the following steps:—
1. Put the first glass in box
2. Put second glass in box
3. Put third glass in box
4. Put lid on filled box
5. Put finished box on "completed pile"

To begin with, Bert is reinforced for merely putting finished boxes on the "completed pile". When he has learned to do this consistently he is required to put the lid on a filled box and then put the finished box on the completed pile to earn his reinforcer.

Next, when this is well learned, he is required to put the third glass in the box (the other two already being in position), put the lid on and put the finished article on the completed pile before being given his reinforcer.

In this way, gradually working backwards, all the steps in the chain are added together until Bert is able to do the entire job.

SUMMARY

The rules for teaching a complex task are:
1. **Break down the task into small simple steps.**
2. **Teach the last step first.**
3. **When that step is well learned, add the second to last step.**
4. **Reinforce *ONLY* after the last step.**
5. **Working *BACKWARDS* gradually add more steps until the whole sequence is learned.**

QUIZ 6
Chaining

Please tick only one answer unless otherwise stated.

1. Most complex tasks are easier to learn if they are:
    (a) Broken down into small, simple steps
    (b) Given with big reinforcers
    (c) Given to the person repeatedly
    (d) Backed up with threats

2. When teaching a complex task it is best to:
    (a) Teach the first step first
    (b) Teach the whole sequence at once
    (c) Teach any step first
    (d) Teach the last step first

3. The person is reinforced:
    (a) At the end of each step
    (b) When he has learned the whole sequence
    (c) At the end of the last step in the chain
    (d) At the end of the first step in the chain

4. Below is a list of the steps involved in removing a sock:
   They are not in the right order. Put the steps in the order in which you take off a sock.

    (a) Remove sock from ankle   1st......................
    (b) Remove sock from toe   2nd......................
    (c) Remove sock from midfoot 3rd......................
    (d) Remove sock from heel   4th......................

5. Which step (a, b, c, or d) would you teach first?   ....

6. After which step (a, b, c, or d) would you always reinforce?   ....

7. How would you, using chaining (and prompting if necessary), teach Louise to complete a five piece jigsaw?
   (You can assume that she will sit for reasonable periods at a table and look at the materials.)

Chapter 7

Maintaining behaviour and coping with difficulties

We have seen that regular reinforcement is the key to teaching behaviour.

Once behaviour is well-learned it does not have to be reinforced every time it happens.

Gradually, the frequency of reinforcement can be reduced until it is given only occasionally.

This is called *intermittent reinforcement*.

Well-learned behaviour, good or bad, will continue to occur regularly as long as it is reinforced intermittently. However, if reinforcement is stopped altogether, even well-learned behaviour will gradually die out. This is called *extinction*.

Intermittent reinforcement maintains behaviour

MAINTAINING BEHAVIOUR

Examples:

Sophie's mother wants her to hang up her coat when she comes in. Every time Sophie hangs up her coat, her mother praises her warmly and hugs her. After a week, Sophie is hanging up her coat every time she is supposed to. Her mother then praises her every other time she hangs up her coat. After another week, Sophie's mother praises her every four times she hangs up her coat. Eventually Sophie's mother only has to praise her now and again.

Notice that Sophie's mother does not stop praising her altogether, but praises her occasionally.

33

Workshop staff are trying to teach Josie to assemble a pedal bin. They teach the task by backward chaining and once the whole task is learned, they simply reinforce Josie every time she assembles a bin. Once they are sure the task is well-learned (i.e. Josie does it consistently without mistakes) the staff *very gradually* reduce the frequency with which they reinforce Josie for assembling bins. To begin with they reinforce Josie nearly every time she makes a bin; a day or two later they may decide to reinforce her for every two bins she assembles. They continue in this way until Josie is reinforced with the same frequency as everyone else in the workshop.

WHEN IN TROUBLE

When teaching isn't working very well, there is something wrong with the programme you are using.

There are several possible reasons why a programme isn't working very well. For example:—

1. You may not be using the right sort of reinforcer. Individuals differ in what they find reinforcing. Also, something that is reinforcing for a person at one time may not be reinforcing at another time. Check that *the reinforcer* you are using is actually s o m e t h i n g t h a t *strengthens* the person's behaviour.

You may not be using the right sort of reinforcers

2. You may not be reinforcing the person enough. You may be asking for too much work for too little reinforcement. Try *increasing the amount* of of reinforcer you use.

You may not be reinforcing the person enough

3. The reinforcer may not be immediate. Check that the reinforcer follows the behaviour you want *as soon as it happens*.
4. You may not be giving the reinforcer often enough. Check that you are reinforcing the behaviour *every time* it happens.
5. The steps you are teaching may be too big. You may have set a target that is too difficult (see Chapter 8). If necessary, break down the task into smaller steps or select a new target that is less difficult.

QUIZ 7
Maintaining Behaviour

Please tick only one answer unless otherwise stated.

1. Once a behaviour has been well-learned you:
   (a) Carry on reinforcing it every time it happens
   (b) Stop reinforcing it
   (c) Reinforce it occasionally
   (d) Gradually reinforce it less and less until you are only reinforcing it occasionally

2. Reducing the frequency of reinforcement is called:
   (a) Extinction
   (b) Chaining
   (c) Intermittent reinforcing
   (d) Shaping

3. If a well-learned behaviour is *NEVER* reinforced it will:
   (a) Continue to happen
   (b) Gradually disappear
   (c) Disappear straight away

4. *NEVER* reinforcing a well-learned behaviour is called:
   (a) Extinction
   (b) Chaining
   (c) Intermittent reinforcing
   (d) Shaping

Section III

PLANNING TEACHING PROGRAMMES

Chapter 8
Deciding what to teach

Before we begin to teach new skills we must collect some simple information about what behaviour already exists.

TEACHING NEW SKILLS
Steps
1. Get a clear picture of the child's skills over the different areas on the *Developmental Checklist* (see page 40).
   In particular make sure the child has the basic skills listed at the beginning of the Checklist. *If not*, these may have to be taught *first*.
2. Choose a new task to teach which is either at the same level on the list, or is at the next level up. When choosing, remember to:
   (a) Select a task which will help balanced development. We want children to learn many different skills, not become very good at just a few.
   (b) Select a task which will quickly be of use to the child and family.
   (c) It is easier to begin teaching if you can find a skill which the child shows interest in learning.
   (d) Don't try and teach too many new skills at once (three new tasks are usually sufficient for intensive teaching).

SELECTING THE TEACHING METHOD

We have already discussed basic teaching using shaping and chaining (see Chapters 5 and 6). Many skills may be taught using either method and it is not possible to lay down hard and fast rules. Generally, if the skill is a fairly simple one, shaping will be used, but if the skill can be broken into many links that can add together, chaining will be best.

Whichever teaching method is used, remember:—
1. Short teaching sessions are better than long ones (10 minutes may be too long in some cases).
2. Regular sessions are important — so choose times when sessions best fit in with everyday life.

Short teaching sessions are better than long ones !

39

3. Keep the steps *SMALL*. If progress stops, try and make steps smaller.
4. Make sure one step is properly mastered before going on to the next.
5. Make sure effective reinforcers are available and that you are using them properly all the time (see Chapter 4).
6. To make sure your teaching is working, it is a good idea to keep progress records (see Chapter 9).

DEVELOPMENTAL CHECKLIST

This checklist is meant to help you to work out what the child can already do and to show you what you can teach him next. It is arranged in the order that children usually learn things. The checklist is split into five main sections with 19 steps in each. The checklist covers what a normal child can do up to about 5 years of age. In fact, many retarded adults will have difficulty in doing some of the things and, thus, the checklist is also applicable to them.

When the person can do all the things on the checklist, you can look at the list of more advanced activities in the Appendix. The activities are in order of difficulty and the ones at the top end are activities that normal adults can do.

HOW TO USE THE DEVELOPMENTAL CHECKLIST

1. On each list, tick the things the child can do. You will have to watch the child to make sure he can do each one. He must do each one without help to get a tick. If he only does it sometimes, he does not get a tick.

2. If the child cannot do something because of a physical handicap, put **H**.

3. Some early steps the child "grows out of", for example, needing to hold on to furniture to stand up. In most cases, if the child can do steps further on, for example, walking, you can assume that he has learned the previous steps and so you can tick them.

Be careful though in areas like social skills, looking at things, and copying and pretending. In these areas a lot of retarded children have big gaps. For example, they look at *things* but not at people. Do not tick these items unless the child does them, or you are sure that he has passed through that stage.

4. When you have been through all the lists, colour in what the child can do on the teaching chart.

    N.B. Do *not* colour in a step unless the child can do all the items in that step.

5. By looking at the chart you will see where the child has gaps and in which areas he needs most help.

6. When you have decided where the child needs most help, look at the *next* item on the list to see what to teach.

7. Teach using the methods described earlier in this book.

Important

There are some things that a child needs to be able to do before he can learn many of the items on the Checklist.

These are:

1. Sits down at a table without fuss.

2.* Looks at you when you call his name.

3. Looks at the object he is working with.

4. Co-operates—that is, he will do what you expect him to do, if he understands what you want and is capable of doing it.
   (You will be able to tell what he understands and can do from the Checklist.)

Tick these if the child can do them. Do *not* tick if he only does them sometimes.

Other systems have been devised to help you choose teaching targets.

For example:—

1. *The Adaptive Behavior Scale:* Obtainable from NFER Publishing Company, 2 Oxford Road East, Windsor, Berks. SL4 1DF.

2. *The Progress Assessment Charts:* Obtainable from N.S.M.H.C. Books, Pembridge Hall, 17 Pembridge Square, London, W2 4EP.

3. *The Adaptive Functioning Index:* Obtainable from Vocational and Rehabilitation Research Institute, 3304, 33 Street, N.W. Calgary, 44, Alberta, Canada.

You may find these useful.

TEACHING CHART

Colour in each step the child can do. Do not colour it in if the child cannot do all the items in that step. If the child cannot do a step because of physical handicap, write H.

Page		STEPS 1 2 3 4 5 6 7 8 9 10 11 12 13 14 15 16 17 18 19
43	MOVEMENT	
44	SOCIAL SKILLS (Getting on with others)	
45	SELF HELP: Drinking and eating	
45	Toileting and washing	
46	Dressing	
47	PLAY: Looking at things and colours	
47	Handling things	
48	Cubes, bricks, formboards and puzzles	
49	Books, paper, crayons and scissors	
49	Action toys, screwing and threading toys	
50	Copying and pretending	
51	LANGUAGE: Understanding	
52	Speech — general conversation	
52	Speech — answers to questions	

42

MOVEMENT

1. Makes crawling movements when lying on stomach.
2. Kicks forcefully.
3. Can bear some weight on legs when held — and lifts foot.
4. Can move head from side to side.
5. Can sit with support — head steady.
6. Can sit in chair briefly.
7. Can bear most weight on legs — when held.
8. Stands with help.
   Sits for one minute or more.
9. Stands holding furniture — cannot lower himself.
   Moves by rolling and squirming on floor.
   Can pull self to sit for 10 minutes.
   Sitting — can lean forward to reach, but not sideways.
10. Pulls and lowers to stand with furniture.
    Sits indefinitely.
11. Walks when led with two hands.
    Walks on hands and feet like a bear.
    Sitting — can twist round to pick up things.
12. Stands alone for a few seconds.
    Walks round furniture and walks when led with one hand.
    Crawls rapidly.
    Can rise to sitting from lying.
13. Walks unsteadily and gets to feet alone.
    Can rise from sitting to standing without support.
    Climbs stairs on hands and knees.
    Kneels without support.
14. Walks well.
    Walks up and down stairs with help.
    Stoops and picks up things from floor without falling.
    Can seat self on chair.
    Can make a few steps sideways and backwards.
15. Runs on whole foot.
    Jumps with both feet.
    Walks up and down stairs — two feet on each step.
    Squats when playing — stands without using hands.
    Pulls chair up to table.
16. Can walk on tiptoe.
    Can cross feet or knees when sitting.
17. Goes upstairs, one foot on each step.
18. Goes downstairs, one foot on each step.
    Hops.
    Picks up objects from floor — bends at waist.
    Marches in time to music.
19. Can walk along a straight line.
    Skips.
    Runs well.

SOCIAL SKILLS (getting on with others)

NOTE: You may not want to teach the items in brackets in the following lists, but they are included because they occur during normal development.

1. Smiles at others when they approach him.
   Quietens when picked up.
   Watches mother when feeding.
2. Smiles and makes noises when talked to.
3. Smiles back at smiling face.
   Shows interest in surroundings — looks around and makes noises.
   Recognises mother — smiles, makes noises, etc. when he sees her.
4. Smiles at people before they approach him.
   Friendly to strangers.
5. Stops crying when talked to.
6. Holds out arms to be picked up.
   Responds to emotional tone of mother's voice.
   Knows who are strangers (e.g. frowns and stares at them).
9. (Needs reassurance before accepting advances of strangers).
10. (Pulls mother's clothes for attention).
12. (Demonstrates affection for familiar people).
    May kiss when asked to.
13. (Moods change quickly).
14. (Dislikes being left).
    (Demands a lot of attention).
15. Plays near but not with other children.
    Plays happily alone, but likes to be with adult.
    Follows adult around.
    (Tantrums when he doesn't get his own way — easily stopped).
16. Watches other children playing — occasionally joins in for a time.
    (Violent tantrums when he doesn't get his own way).
17. Joins in play with other children.
    Creates own play — plays on his own happily for some time.
    Recognises sex differences: tells you who is a boy, who is a girl.
    Separates from mother easily.
    (Affectionate and confiding).
    Able to tidy up toys if encouraged.
    Shares toys, sweets, etc.
18. Takes turns.
    Plays in small group of children.
    Performs for others, e.g. recites, dances, etc.
    Goes on short distance errands, e.g. to neighbours.
    (General behaviour self-willed).
    (Needs friends of his own age).
19. Follows group rules.
    Plays competitive exercise games.
    (Tantrums much less frequent).
    (Chooses own friends).

SELF HELP
Eating and drinking
1. Sucks well.
2. Shows anticipation when about to be fed.
5. Pats bottle.
   Holds bottle.
6. Drinks from cup when held to lips.
   Holds spoon with help.
   Sucks soft food off spoon.
   Chews and eats biscuit when fed with it.
7. Keeps lips closed when offered more food than he wants.
9. Helps to hold cup for drinking.
   Feeds self with biscuit.
   Rubs spoon across plate.
10. (Finger feeds).
12. Drinks from cup with a little help.
    Holds spoon — cannot use it alone.
13. Manages cup up and down without much spilling.
    Holds spoon, brings to mouth and licks, but spoon tends to rotate.
    Chews well — some mess.
    Can manage to eat food on his own, but messily.
14. Uses cup with both hands.
    Spoon no longer rotates.
    Hands empty dish to mother.
    Discriminates edible substances (doesn't eat rubbish, may bite objects, but no need to watch him).
15. Uses cup with one hand — no spilling.
    Pours from one cup to another.
    Uses spoon competently.
    Chews competently.
    Removes wrapper from sweet before eating.
16. Sucks through straw.
    Gets drink unassisted, e.g. water, milk.
    Uses fork — not very well.
17. Pours from jug.
    Eats with spoon and fork — messy.
    Handles breakable objects.
18. Eats skilfully with spoon and fork.
    Beginning to use knife and fork.
19. Uses knife and fork.
    Spreads with knife.
    Prepares simple foods, e.g. jelly.

Toileting and Washing
3. Enjoys bath.
10. Shows discomfort when wet or soiled.

12. Gives some indication of need for toilet.
    Plays with flannel and toys in the bath.
13. Regularity — usually urinates when sat on pot or toilet at a regular time.
    Sometimes asks for pot or toilet.
14. Dry by day, occasional accidents.
    (Urgency over urine passing).
15. Tells you his toilet needs in reasonable time.
    Goes to toilet by self for bowels.
    Dry at night if lifted in the evening.
    Attempts to soap and wash self in the bath.
16. Goes to toilet by self for urine.
    Pulls off pants at toilet — seldom replaces.
    Climbs onto toilet seat.
    Inadequate attempt to wash hands.
    Dries hands acceptably if reminded.
17. Attends to toilet needs without help except for wiping.
    Dry by night.
    Dries hands well.
18. Attends to toilet needs fully — wipes, washes and dries hands well.
    Brushes teeth.
19. Washes face well.
    Washing, apart from face and hands, requires help.
    Tidies hair occasionally.

Dressing

11. Holds out arm for sleeve, or foot for shoe.
12. Takes off socks.
    Helps with dressing — holding out limbs.
13. Takes off shoes.
14. Unzips.
15. Takes off pants, coat and dress. (May be unfastened for him).
    Puts on shoes, socks and pants.
16. Unbuttons front buttons.
17. Undresses fully except back fastenings.
    Puts on coat.
    Attempts to fasten button.
    Partially dresses self if reminded.
18. Dresses and undresses except for back fastenings.
    Can fasten buttons.
    Puts on vest and tight T-shirt.
19. Laces shoes and ties laces.
    Dresses and undresses without help.

PLAY
Looking at things and colours
(The four primary colours are red, blue, green and yellow. Matching a colour means putting something of one colour with something of the same colour—nothing need be said.)
1. Eyes follow object dangled in front of face. Looks at face briefly.
2. Eyes follow a moving person.
3. Eyes follow object moving from side to side. Looks at own hands intently.
   Eyes focus on near object.
   Looks steadily at faces.
4. Looks at dropped object.
5. Looks at object on table.
   Smiles at himself in mirror.
6. Eyes move in unison (no longer stares at hands).
7. Pats image of himself in mirror.
   Will change his position to see an object not in front of him.
9. Looks for an object hidden while watching.
10. Looks round a corner for object.
11. Points at objects through glass.
12. Looks for and finds an object hidden before his eyes.
14. Points at distant objects out of doors.
16. Matches one primary colour.
17. Matches two primary colours.
18. Matches four primary colours.
    Names four primary colours.
19. Matches ten colours.
    Names six colours.
    Matches different shapes.

Handling things
2. Holds rattle for a very short time.
3. Grasps hold of an object when it is placed in his hand.
   Shakes rattle for a very short time.
   Plays with own hands.
4. Shakes rattle for long periods of time.
5. Will grasp objects on his own.
   Pats objects.
   Uses either hand to reach for objects.
6. Reaches for objects.
   Can transfer objects from one hand to the other.
   When drops objects, forgets them.
7. Shakes rattle hard.
   Bangs objects on table.
   Usually uses preferred hand to reach for objects (i.e. he is right handed or left handed).

8. Strikes objects with other objects.
   Pulls string to get an object.
9. Pokes objects with index finger (first finger).
   Picks objects up with index finger and thumb instead of whole hand.
   Throws objects on floor on purpose.
   Offers object to you, but will not let it go.
10. Reaches for toys and explores them with his hands.
12. Throws objects on floor again and again.
    Gives objects to you when you ask — sometimes gives them without you asking.
13. Picks up small objects neatly.
14. Uses a stick to get an object that is out of his reach.
15. Is definitely right-handed or left-handed.
16. Folds a piece of paper in half. Can move fingers separately.
18. Cuts paper into 3 equal squares.
19. Can sew roughly.
    Can tie a knot at the end of thread.
    Makes models with playdough or plasticene.

Cubes, bricks, formboards and puzzles
(A formboard is a tray with pieces you can take out. A puzzle is cut-up pieces that you can put together.)

6. If he is holding one cube, will drop it when you offer him another.
7. If he is holding one cube will hold on to it when you offer him another.
9. Holds 2 cubes with both hands.
12. Puts cubes in a box.
13. Holds 2 cubes in one hand.
    Builds a 2-cube tower.
    Puts round block in round hole in formboard.
14. Builds a 4-cube tower.
    Puts round and square blocks in round and square holes in formboard.
15. Does simple 3-piece formboard.
    Puts large pegs in peg-board.
16. Builds an 8-cube tower.
    Does 2-piece jigsaw puzzle.
17. Builds a 10-cube tower.
    Does 3 — 4-piece jigsaw puzzle.
18. Copies a 3-cube pyramid. (That is, if you build one first, he will copy yours).
    Builds simple things with *Lego*.
    Does 4 — 8-piece jigsaw puzzle.
19. Plans and builds constructively (builds house with *Lego*).
    Does 12-piece jigsaw puzzle.

Books, paper, crayons and scissors
5. Crumples paper in hands.
12. Looks at pictures in book.
    Holds crayon or pencil in fist.
13. Pats picture in book.
    Helps turn pages.
    Copies straight scribble.
14. Enjoys simple picture book.
    Will point to coloured parts of picture when you ask (for example, "Show me the ball").
    Turns several pages together.
    Scribbles using preferred hand (he is right-handed, or left-handed).
15. Turns pages one by one.
    Will point to detailed items when you ask (e.g., "Show me the girl's hair".)
    Copies vertical and circular scribble.
16. Copies horizontal scribble.
    Beginning to draw on his own.
    Folds paper.
    Holds scissors clumsily — beginning to cut.
17. Draws a man with head and one other part.
    Paints with large brush and easel.
    Cuts out pictures — not very accurately.
18. Matches pictures.
    Copies a cross.
    Uses scissors with ease.
    Draws a simple house.
19. Copies a triangle and letters.
    Draws a recognisable man.
    Using scissors — can cut along a line.
    Can cut cloth.

Action toys, screwing and threading toys
12. Pushes little cars.
    Rolls ball to adult.
13. Pushes large wheeled toys.
    Rolls ball on his own.
14. Strings cotton reels.
15. Throws and kicks ball.
    Strings large beads (one inch).
    Throws ball into basket.
16. Turns door-knobs and screws lids.
17. Plays on the floor with cars, bricks etc.
    Climbs nursery apparatus well.
    Uses pedal on tricycle.
    Strings small beads (half an inch).

18. Climbs ladders and trees.
    Catches large ball.
19. Uses slides and swings.
    Can use hammer.
    Can wind fairly evenly onto a spool.
    Uses screwdriver.
    Can use saw.

Copying and pretending

1. Looks at faces for a short while.
   Stares at mother's face when she is talking to or feeding him.
2. Smiles and makes noises when talked to.
3. Looks at surroundings with interest.
   Focusses eyes on a near object.
   Looks at object in front of him straight away.
   Shows anticipation when about to be fed or lifted (for example, opens his mouth when he sees food, holds out his arms when mother holds out hers).
4. Pulls dress over face.
5. Smiles at himself in mirror.
6. Laughs when his head is hidden (for example, under a towel).
   Copies you if you cough or stick your tongue out at him.
7. Copies very simple acts and noises (for example, arm waving, "goo-gooing").
   Enjoys "peepbo", but does not yet play himself.
   Pats image of himself in mirror.
8. Copies you shaking a rattle, ringing a bell, etc.
9. Copies hand-clapping.
10. Plays "pat-a-cake".
    Waves "Bye-bye" when shown.
12. Plays "Peepbo" covering his face.
    Knows what body movement is coming next when nursery rhymes are said.
    Plays up and down games.
13. Begins to copy mother doing housework.
14. Briefly copies simple action (for example, kissing a doll, reading a book).
    Copies mother washing, dusting and cleaning.
15. Pretending play begins (for example, making a toy animal walk).
    Plays copying mother's domestic tasks (for example, putting a doll to bed).
17. Can copy closing fist and wiggling thumb.
18. Strong dramatic play and dressing-up (for example, being a nurse).
    Sometimes has a pretend friend.
19. Acts stories out in detail.

LANGUAGE
Understanding

1. Watches mother closely when she speaks.
3. Turns towards a nearby voice or meaningful sound.
   Shows distress through a loud sound.
4. Excites on hearing steps; that is, he makes noises and movements.
   Looks straight at bell, rattle, etc., when he hears it.
   Responds to emotional tone of mother's voice (for example, cries when she sounds cross, laughs when she sounds happy).
8. Stops what he is doing for a short while when you say "No".
9. Listens to wristwatch or clock.
10. Responds to some words (for example, looks or points when you say "Where's Daddy?").
12. Immediately turns to his own name.
    Understands and obeys simple commands with gesture (for example, "Give me . . .", "Wave Bye-bye").
    Comes when called.
    Goes to points directed.
13. Understands and obeys simple commands without gesture (for example, "Shut the door"; "Give me the ball"; "Get your shoes").
    Points to familiar persons, toys, etc. when asked.
14. Follows directions (for example, "Put the doll on the chair").
    Shows own or doll's hair, shoes, etc. when asked.
    Pictures — points to one named thing.
15. Points to five parts of doll or self.
    Shows 3 objects or pictures when asked.
    (Prepositions are words l:e *in, on, under, behind, beside,* **etc.**)
    Can carry out two different prepositions when you ask him (for example, "Put the cup *under* the table", "Put the car *in* the box").
16. Shows you objects when you describe them by their use (for example, "What do we cut with?").
    If asked to pass *one*, does not pass more.
17. Listens to short story.
    Gives two out of many.
18. Can carry out four different prepositions when asked.
    Can show you which is the longer of two lines.
    Can show you which is the big one and the small one of two objects (for example, two cups).
19. Can carry out a triple order preposition (for example, "Put the spoon *in* the cup, put the cup *under* the table and then sit *on* the chair").

Speech — general conversation

1. Makes throaty noises.
   "Coos" when happy.
2. Says "Ah, eh, oh".
3. Says most vowel sounds, "Ah, eh, oh, uh, ih".
4. Laughs aloud.
5. Says "Ahgoo".
6. Grunts and growls.
   Says single and double syllables.
   Screams when annoyed.
7. Says "da, ka, ba, ga".
8. Says "dada, baba".
9. Babbles (syllables, not words).
   Shouts to attract attention.
10. Shakes head for "No".
12. Asks for objects by pointing.
    Tries to sing.
13. Speaks 2 — 6 words.
    Uses gesture to make his wants known.
    Uses one word to cover several words (e.g. "dada" is all men).
14. Speaks 6 — 20 words.
    Echoes prominent or last word said to him.
15. Speaks 50+ words.
    Echoes many words.
    Talks continuously to himself when playing.
    Speaks his food and toilet needs.
    Speaks 2-word sentences.
16. Speaks 200+ words.
    Uses pronouns: I, me, you.
    Combines two ideas (for example, "Daddy gone", "More chocolate").
    Uses plurals.
    Says 3-word sentences.
17. Carries on simple conversation.
    Asks what, where, who.
    Says 4-word sentences.
18. Uses conjunctions like: and, but, so, etc.
19. Can tell you a connected account of recent things that have happened to him.

Speech — answers to questions

8. Copies sounds (for example, "ooh, uuh").
12. Copies animal noises that you make (for example, "meow, woof").
    Tries to copy words.

15. Gives first name.
    Shows and repeats hair, eyes, shoes, etc.
    Names 2 — 3 objects in picture book.
    Names 3 — 5 objects.
17. Gives full name and sex.
    May count up to 10 (without objects to count).
    Answers simple questions (for example, "What did you have for breakfast?").
    Repeats two numbers you say to him (for example "6, 8").
18. Gives address and age.
    Counts three objects placed in front of him.
    Listens to and tells simple stories.
    Can repeat three numbers you say to him (for example, "3, 9, 2").
    Can explain simple concepts, like toys, animals, food, etc. (for example, "You can eat food", "Toys are things you play with").
    Can tell you what to do when hungry, cold, etc. (for example, "When you are cold, you put on your coat").
    Can tell you what day of the week it is.
    Enjoys jokes.
    Can tell you what simple things are made of (for example, table of wood).
19. Gives birthday.
    Counts five fingers on one hand.
    Can tell you whether it is morning or afternoon.
    Repeats four numbers you say to him.
    Defines some simple words (for example, "A ball is round, it bounces, and you play with it"; "A dog is an animal with four legs which barks").
    Can name days of the week in order.
    Can tell you which is longer of day/week, hour/minute, etc.
    Can tell you the month and the year.
    Tells left and right on himself.

QUIZ 8

Deciding what to teach and developmental checklist

Tick only one answer unless otherwise stated.

1. When using the Developmental Checklist, should you:
    (a) Ask someone who knows the child, what the child can do
    (b) Tick items the child can do when he wants to
    (c) Watch the child and only tick items you see he can do without help
    (d) Tick items the child requires occasional help with.

2. There are four things the child may need to learn before you teach anything on the Developmental Checklist. They are:
    (a) ....
    (b) ....
    (c) ....
    (d) ....

3. When deciding what to teach you look at the teaching chart and:
    (a) Choose a task in an area the child is good at, to build on his skills
    (b) See where the child has gaps and teach one of these
    (c) Teach something out of each area
    (d) Always start with self-help skills

4. Teaching sessions are best if they are:
    (a) As long as possible
    (b) At any time of the day
    (c) At least every other day
    (d) Short and regular

Chapter 9

Keeping Records

Once you have chosen a teaching target, you need to start keeping records.

The records you keep will depend on the type of target you have chosen. There are two main types—"How often?" records and "How long?" records.

"HOW OFTEN?" RECORDS

"How often?" records are used to record the frequency with which an event occurs.

For example, you might want to record HOW OFTEN someone does the washing up after tea, or HOW OFTEN he comes when you call him.

Example:
  The target is to teach Evan to do the washing up after tea without a reminder.
  The first stage is to find out HOW OFTEN he does it now.

  A record sheet like this would be useful:

Date	Does he do the washing up without a reminder?
Mon. 3rd July	Yes
Tues. 4th July	No
Wed. 5th July	No
Thurs. 6th July	Yes

In this example, Evan does the task on only half the occasions.
Once you started the teaching plan, you would look for gradual improvement. If Evan didn't make progress, you would need to revise the teaching plan.

"HOW LONG" RECORDS

"How long?" records are used to record the length of time an event lasts.

For example, you might decide to record HOW LONG someone sits at the meal-table or HOW LONG he plays without throwing something.

Example:
  The target is to teach Amy to sit at the tea table for longer periods.

The first stage is to find out HOW LONG she sits at the table before getting up now.

A record sheet like this would be useful:

Name: AMY
Date: 3rd October

Sat down at	Got up at	How long?
5.05 p.m.	5.09 p.m.	4 mins.
5.12 p.m.	5.15 p.m.	3 mins.
5.21 p.m.	5.26 p.m.	5 mins.
5.27 p.m.	5.31 p.m.	4 mins.

From these records, it is clear that Amy sits, on average, for only four minutes before leaving the tea table. Once the teaching plan was started, you would look for gradual progress. If progress did not occur, the teaching plan would need revision.

Of course, records can be much more complicated than this. This is often so when you are teaching the person something completely new.

Then, it often helps to record HOW MUCH HELP the person needs to do the task.

Example:

The target is to teach Ben to put on his vest.

Before starting to teach Ben, it is a good idea to see how much he can do for himself.

You have broken down the task into simple steps and you let Ben try each step alone. If he cannot do it without help, you help him but give as little help as possible.

Use a gestural prompt *only* if a verbal prompt alone has not worked. Use a physical prompt *only* if gestural and verbal prompts have not worked.

A useful record sheet might look like this:

Name: BEN

	Monday	Tuesday	Wednesday
Picks up vest	√	√	√
Puts right arm in hole	√	√	√
Puts left arm in hole	√	√	√
Pulls vest over head	V G	V G	V G
Pulls vest down to waist	V G P	V G P	V G P

P = physical prompt needed
G = gestural prompt needed
V = verbal prompt needed
√ = No help needed

In this case, Ben can do the first three steps without help.

However, he needs verbal and gestural prompts to pull the vest over his head and he needs verbal, gestural and physical prompts to pull it down to his waist.

Your teaching plan might attempt to fade out these prompts, starting with the physical prompt needed at the last step.

WHY BOTHER TO KEEP RECORDS?

There are three main reasons for keeping records.

1. Records help you to work out your teaching plan.
   When working out a teaching plan you need to find out exactly what the person can do.
   Obviously, the way you teach a task to someone will depend on how much of the task he can already do for himself. Keeping records to find out more about what the person can do, so that you can work out your teaching plan, is called "getting a baseline."

2. Records help you to see whether your teaching is working.
   Progress is sometimes slow. Records let you see small improvements that you might otherwise miss. Records can also help you to decide how to improve your teaching plan.

3. Records keep other people informed.
   Records show other people how you are getting on. They also let them know what they are meant to do if they are helping you.

Records show how you are getting on

PRACTICAL POINTS

The best records are simple but give you enough facts to plan your teaching.

It is a good idea to use a clipboard so that records do not get lost.

SUMMARY

1. The two main types of records are:
   (a) "How often?" records
   (b) "How long?" records.
2. Records help you work out your teaching plan.
3. Records help you see whether your teaching is working.
4. Records keep other people informed of progress.
5. Records should help teaching, not take up all your time.

QUIZ 9

Please tick only one answer per question unless otherwise stated.

1. The two *main* types of record are:
   (a) How quickly and how much
   (b) How well and how long
   (c) How long and how often
   (d) How easily and how quickly

2. Indicate the sort of record you would keep for *each* of the following targets:

Put 'O' for how often and 'L' for how long.

   (a) You want to teach Martin to obey "Come here". At the moment he does not always come when called. ....
   (b) You want to improve Michael's work. At the moment he keeps stopping for a chat or a "day dream". ....
   (c) You want to teach Brenda to catch a ball when you throw it to her. At the moment she often drops it. ....
   (d) You want to teach Liz to play outside on the swing. At the moment she only goes on it for a little while. ....
   (e) You want to teach Margaret to make her bed every morning. She hardly ever does at the moment. ....
   (f) You want to teach Peter to wash his hands after using the toilet. He rarely does this at the moment. ....
   (g) You want Joe to get from the training centre to his home more quickly. ....

Section IV

COPING WITH PROBLEM BEHAVIOUR

Chapter 10

Causes of problem behaviour and recording problem behaviour

The most important thing to remember about problem behaviour is that *PROBLEM BEHAVIOUR IS LEARNED AND MAINTAINED IN THE SAME WAY AS ANY OTHER BEHAVIOUR — IT IS REINFORCED.*

Examples :

Philip has been sitting in the day room on his ward watching T.V. There is nothing else to do and, whilst he is behaving well, no one pays any attention to him.

He climbs onto his chair and starts to jump up and down, screaming and biting himself. Immediately, a nurse comes over to see what's happening, talks to him (maybe even tells him off or shouts at him) and gets him down from the chair.

In the future Philip will be more likely to jump on the furniture, screaming and biting himself, because he is reinforced with attention from the nurse for doing so.

When Jane and her mother go shopping, Jane starts playing up in the supermarket. Mother buys Jane some sweets to keep her quiet. Jane will be more likely to play up next time she's in the supermarket because she's been reinforced with sweets for doing so.

Problem behaviour is learned because it is reinforced

Most problem behaviour is reinforced *intermittently* and hence keeps happening.

Examples :

Joe keeps approaching strangers in the hospital and asking them for cigarettes. Usually they ignore him but occasionally they stop and talk to him, sometimes giving him a cigarette.

Joe's behaviour is maintained by *intermittent reinforcers* — conversation with strangers and cigarettes.

Mary steals food from other people's plates. Usually the staff see her in time to stop her. Occasionally, however, they miss her and she gets extra to eat. Mary's food stealing is *intermittently reinforced* by food.

Why is it so easy to reinforce bad behaviour?

Telling someone off when he misbehaves usually interrupts the behaviour for a while. So, the person giving the telling off thinks it is working. This is probably reinforcing for him and hence he will be more likely to tell off the other person in future. Telling off often seems to work in the short run, but it often makes things worse in the long run.

Example :

There are ten trainees in the workshop. They are packing light fittings. Every now and then one of them stands up. Mr. Bloggs, the supervisor, immediately shouts "Sit down!" and finds that he is obeyed. Over the next few days he finds, to his surprise, that his trainees gradually stand up more and more often until they hardly spend any time sitting down working.

In fact, shouting "Sit down!" has taught the trainees that, if they stand up, they get attention. Mr. Bloggs has reinforced standing up by mistake — although he thought he was teaching the trainees to sit down!

No one deliberately teaches bad behaviour — it is taught accidentally. But we can see from these examples that problem behaviour is learned and maintained in the same way as good behaviour — *it is reinforced.*

RECORDING PROBLEM BEHAVIOUR

We know that problem behaviour is learned and that it continues because the person is reinforced for behaving that way — even if the reinforcement is only occasional.

Therefore, when recording problem behaviour we must find out what is reinforcing it. Besides noting how often the problem occurs — and/or how long it lasts — we must also find out what is reinforcing it, by observing exactly what happens immediately afterwards.

It also helps to know if there is a *"green light"* for problem behaviour. For example, does it occur in certain places, at certain times or with certain people? Recording what happens just before the behaviour should help you find out. Good records also tell you how much progress you are making in changing the behaviour.

Chart for Peter — see first example overleaf

DATE	TIME	WHAT WAS HAPPENING BEFORE?	WHAT DID PETER DO?	WHAT HAPPENED AFTER?
16th Dec.	11.40	Putting toys away in cupboard.	Hit Jimmy twice.	Teacher told him off and tried to reason with him.
	3.00	Sitting down having drinks. Peter had finished his.	Hit Jimmy once and said "Drink".	Teacher gave him a drink.
	3.10	Playing on climbing frame.	Hit Jimmy once.	Jimmy hit him back.

Chart for Lisa — see second example overleaf

DATE	TIME	WHAT HAPPENED BEFORE?	HOW LONG DID TANTRUM LAST?	WHAT HAPPENED AFTERWARDS?
12th Jan.	7.30	Told time for bed.	35 secs.	Told she could stay and watch 10 more minutes T.V. Quietened down.
12th Jan.	7.40	Told to go to bed.	45 secs.	Smacked and taken to bed. Still screaming.

63

Examples:
  Peter hits his little brother and we want to stop this. You could use a chart, like the one on the previous page, to record:
  (a) How often this happens each day.
  (b) What Peter and his brother were doing beforehand, i.e. Is there a "green light?"
  (c) Exactly what happened afterwards, i.e., What's reinforcing it?

  Lisa lies on the floor and screams when told it is time for bed. You could record how often she does this, how long it lasts and what happens before and afterwards on a chart like the one shown.

  Some problem behaviour, by its nature, has to be interrupted quickly, for example, where a child is in danger of harming himself or other people. It is still important in understanding the reasons for the behaviour to record as much information as possible. It may be important to note where it occurs (e.g., only in shops), or in whose presence (e.g., only when Dad is present/absent).

  Keeping records will show if the behaviour is getting better. It is important, when looking at records, to remember that much problem behaviour will get *worse* at the start of a programme, before it begins to get better (see Chapter 13).

"GREEN LIGHTS" AND BAD BEHAVIOUR

  People learn to behave badly in some situations and not in others. In other words, bad behaviour can have a "green light". In the examples above, Philip's "green light" is the dayroom which has no staff in it. He has learned that if he misbehaves in this situation he is reinforced with attention. Jane's "green light" is the supermarket. She has learned that she is reinforced with sweets if she plays up in this situation.

  Joe's "green light" is a stranger and Mary's "green light" is food on nearby plates. Both have learned that problem behaviour in these situations earns them reinforcement.

  What we need to do is change these "green lights" into "red lights" for bad behaviour and "green lights" for good behaviour. The next few chapters discuss ways in which this can be done.

QUIZ 19

The causes of problem behaviour

Please tick only one answer unless otherwise stated.

1. Problem behaviour is:
   (a) Caused by emotional disturbance
   (b) Inherited
   (c) Caused by brain damage and illness
   (d) Learned

2. Jack bangs his head because:
   - (a) He has toothache
   - (b) He's reinforced for headbanging
   - (c) He's trying to communicate
   - (d) He's jealous of other children

3. John takes off his clothes ten times a day because:
   - (a) He's hot
   - (b) He's frustrated
   - (c) He's retarded
   - (d) He's reinforced for doing so

4. Problem behaviour is maintained by:
   - (a) Intermittent reinforcement
   - (b) Emotional conflict
   - (c) The ward or home atmosphere
   - (d) Mental illness

5. Everytime the patients misbehave in the day room the nurse bangs on the office window and shouts at them. If attention from the nurse is reinforcing they will be more likely to:
   - (a) Stop misbehaving altogether
   - (b) Carry on misbehaving
   - (c) Stop misbehaving briefly but misbehave more often in the future
   - (d) Gradually stop misbehaving.

6. At tea-time Gerald screams unless he is served straight away. His mother serves him as soon as he starts to scream to keep him quiet. What will happen now and in the future? What is the "green light" for misbehaviour?

   ....
   ....
   ....

7. Derek bites his fingers when he is in the classroom. You want to stop this — what records would you keep?

Chapter 11

Will punishment work?

Punishment is following behaviour with an unpleasant event like a "telling off", a smack or a fine. It is often used to stop us from doing things we are not supposed to. It sometimes works. It is not a good way of coping with problem behaviour in the retarded because:

Firstly, punishment *does not teach a person what to do*. It only teaches him what not to do.

Secondly, a smack or a "telling off" means *giving the person attention*. This attention may sometimes reinforce the bad behaviour and make it worse. This is more likely if the person has no opportunity to get attention for good behaviour.

Thirdly, punishment also often *loses its effectiveness*. It may make problem behaviour happen less often for a while but often the problem will gradually come back again.

For these and other reasons, punishment is *not* a good way of coping with problem behaviour in retarded people.

The most important step when looking at problem behaviour is to make sure that we *teach good behaviour* which can be reinforced. This is particularly true when working with retarded people who find much learning difficult.

SUMMARY

1. Punishment *never* teaches a person what to do; it can at best only teach what not to do.
2. A smack or telling off means giving the person attention. Often this *attention is reinforcing* and makes the problem behaviour worse.
3. Punishment can often gradually *lose its effectiveness.*
4. The first thing to do in coping with problem behaviour, is to *teach good behaviour* which can be reinforced.

QUIZ 11
Will punishment work?

Please tick only one answer unless otherwise stated.

1. Punishment is following behaviour with: (a) A nice event (b) Nothing (c) An unpleasant event (d) A reinforcer
2. Punishment is a way of teaching someone good behaviour. True or False.
3. Punishment sometimes reinforces bad behaviour because it involves attention. True or False.
4. Punishers often lose their effectiveness. True or False.
5. Punishment is unpleasant for all concerned. True or False.
6. Punishment should always be used to deal with problem behaviour. True or False.

Chapter 12

First steps in coping with problem behaviour

We have seen that punishment is a bad way of dealing with problem behaviour. We have also seen that, often, bad behaviour is the only way a person can earn reinforcement.

Hence, the main thing to do is to teach the person that good *behaviour will earn reinforcers.*
REINFORCERS MUST ALWAYS BE AVAILABLE FOR GOOD BEHAVIOUR.
In some cases the good behaviour may have to be taught.

Examples:

Remember Jane? She played up in the supermarket until Mum bought her sweets to keep her quiet.

The first thing Mum did was teach Jane to help with the shopping (fetching things from the shelves, naming products, pushing the trolley and so on). She reinforced improving behaviour with lots of praise and attention and the occasional sweet.

Mum found that Jane was much better behaved when she could earn reinforcement for good behaviour.

Remember Philip? He was the boy who jumped up and down on chairs, screaming and biting himself to get staff attention.

The first thing the ward staff did was to get together and see how Philip spent his day. Most of his day was spent sitting around doing nothing. He very rarely got any attention for good behaviour. The

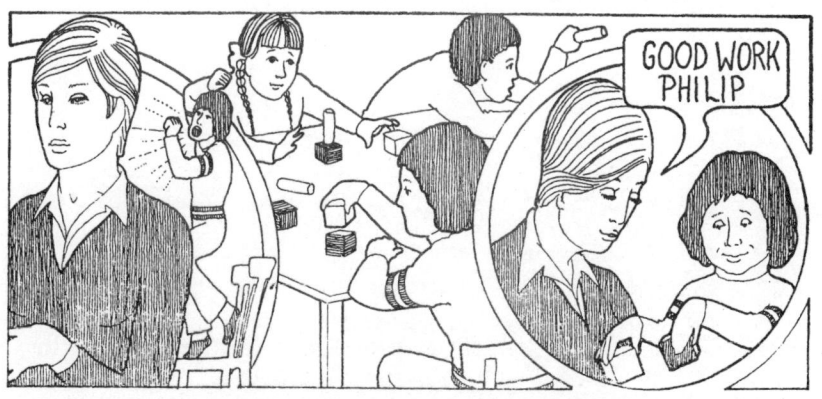

Philip is reinforced only when he behaves well

staff decided that Philip should join a group of residents who were learning simple skills, like doing puzzles, building with *Lego*, threading beads, etc.

Philip was not very good at these tasks to start off with and so shaping was done. Lots of praise and attention was used to reinforce gradual improvement.

The staff found that, not only did Philip's skills get better, but he was much less likely to misbehave because he could earn attention from staff with good behaviour.

The workshops were short of jobs one morning and so a group of trainees was sitting doing nothing. Gradually, the behaviour of the whole group deteriorated. Trainees began to fight, argue, tease each other, bob up and down out of their seats, and so on.

The workshop staff decided that they ought to give the trainees a chance to earn attention for appropriate behaviour. So, they got together some simple puzzles and toys and, whenever they ran out of work, gave these to their trainees. They made a special point of always making a fuss of trainees who were occupying themselves properly. They found that, because the trainees could earn reinforcement with good behaviour, they were much less likely to misbehave.

In each of these examples we are trying to make the situation (e.g. the supermarket, dayroom, or workshop) a "green light" for good rather than bad behaviour.

SUMMARY

The main thing to do when dealing with problem behaviour is to make sure the person is getting lots of reinforcement for good behaviour. If he is behaving well there is less time for him to behave badly.

QUIZ 12
First steps

Please tick only one answer for questions 1 and 2.

1. The main thing to do when eliminating problem behaviour is:
    (a) Punish it
    (b) Reinforce it
    (c) Make sure good behaviour is reinforced
    (d) Tell the person off
2. If you reinforce good behaviour:
    (a) The bad behaviour gets worse
    (b) The bad behaviour is reduced and good behaviour is taught
    (c) Bad behaviour is reduced
    (d) Good behaviour is taught

3. Gerry doesn't spend much time playing properly. He tends to climb on furniture, bang on windows and throw toys about the room. What are the first steps you should take to deal with these problems?

....

....

....

Chapter 13

Extinction

We have seen that reinforcement of *good* behaviour is the most important part of dealing with problem behaviour. We know that problem behaviour is usually reinforced intermittently and that this is what keeps it going.

You will remember from Chapter 7 that behaviour disappears if it is never reinforced. Hence if we want to eliminate problem behaviour we must make sure that it is *never* reinforced. This is called *extinction*. During extinction the behaviour often gets worse at first before it gradually dies out.

There are several ways to make sure that problem behaviour is never reinforced. The one you choose depends on what sort of reinforcers are keeping the problem behaviour going.

You must first study the records of the problem behaviour and work out what is reinforcing it. The reinforcer will be something that happens *after* the problem behaviour although it may not follow the problem behaviour every time it happens.

Once you have spotted the reinforcer you must try and work out how you can make sure it *never* follows the behaviour.

THINGS ARE BETTER SINCE WE ALWAYS IGNORE HIS SILLY TALK.

To eliminate problem behaviour, it should NEVER be reinforced

SUMMARY

1. Problem behaviour is maintained by intermittent reinforcement.
2. We must make sure problem behaviour is *never* reinforced. This is called *extinction*.
3. The method you use to extinguish problem behaviour depends on the type of reinforcer that is keeping the problem behaviour going.
4. You should be able to spot the reinforcers from your records of what follows the problem behaviour.

QUIZ 13
Extinction

Please tick only one answer unless otherwise stated.

1. Extinction is:
    (a) Stopping all reinforcement
    (b) Stopping most reinforcement
    (c) Punishment
    (d) Occasional reinforcement

2. During extinction:
    (a) Bad behaviour stops immediately
    (b) Bad behaviour is maintained
    (c) Bad behaviour stops gradually
    (d) Bad behaviour increases at first then gradually stops

3. The reinforcer that maintains problem behaviour usually:
    (a) Comes before the behaviour sometimes
    (b) Follows the behaviour everytime it happens
    (c) Follows the behaviour sometimes
    (d) Comes before the behaviour everytime it happens

4. The technique you use to extinguish problem behaviour is always the same: True or False.

Chapter 14

Some methods of extinction

IGNORING PROBLEM BEHAVIOUR

Sometimes problem behaviour is reinforced by the attention it earns for the person who is misbehaving. With this sort of behaviour, one way to make sure it is never reinforced is to *ignore it completely every time it happens*. Of course, you would make sure that good behaviour was *always* reinforced.

Examples:

Jake was continually approaching staff and tugging at their clothes. The staff got together and kept records of the behaviour. They decided that this irritating behaviour was being maintained by attention and agreed to ignore it *EVERY TIME* it happened. At the same time, of course, staff made sure that attention could be earned for appropriate behaviour.

At first, Jake tugged at their clothes even more but when he found he *NEVER* got attention for doing so the problem behaviour gradually died out.

The staff decided to ignore Jake's annoying behaviour whenever it occurred

Rose used to rush around the living room at home, jumping on furniture and so on. Her parents would tell her to stop rushing about and sit down. Whilst Rose was sitting quietly, her parents would get on with the housework or watch T.V.

Gradually Rose spent more and more time running around, jumping on furniture. Looking at records they had kept, the parents realised they were reinforcing this bad behaviour with attention. Hence, they decided to make sure that they *NEVER* paid attention to Rose when she was rushing about.

At first Rose rushed about even more but, when she learned that she never got attention by doing this, she did so less and less. Of course, Rose's parents made sure she got lots of fuss and attention when she was sitting quietly. They also made sitting quietly reinforcing, by giving Rose lots of puzzles and toys to play with when she was sitting down.

TIME-OUT FROM REINFORCEMENT

Sometimes, it is very difficult to make sure that behaviour is ignored. For example, although staff may ignore problem behaviour, it may be reinforced by classmates or other residents paying attention to it.

Also, some behaviour may be so dangerous that it must be stopped, for example, kicking and biting others or breaking windows.

In these situations, *TIME-OUT* may work best. Time-Out works as follows:
1. When the person misbehaves you say "No". *Once only.*
2. You then *immediately* put the person somewhere alone where he will receive no reinforcement.
3. He remains there for 3 minutes.
4. After 3 minutes he is allowed back, if he is behaving himself.
5. If he is still misbehaving, you wait until he is quiet for 20 seconds or so and then allow him back.

Time-out is one way of removing reinforcers

Time-Out is simply a way of making sure that problem behaviour is *never* followed by a reinforcer. Therefore, it should be *immediate*. There should be no threats or scolding; the person should simply be taken directly to the Time-Out area.

The Time-Out area should be:
1. *Boring*: It must not be reinforcing in any way.
2. *Safe*: There should be no windows or pipes which could hurt someone during a tantrum.
3. *Well lit and ventilated*.
4. *Observable*: You should be able to see (i) that the person is safe and (ii) when he has quietened down.

Examples:

Julie used to bang her hand hard against the window. This was a good way to get attention because her mother didn't feel she could safely ignore such dangerous behaviour. She would approach Julie, tell her off and move her away from the window.

Julie's window-banging behaviour was reinforced by her mother's attention.

Mother decided to use Time-Out. Every time Julie banged the window her mother said "No", and immediately excluded her from the room.

Mother kept an eye on her and, after three minutes, provided Julie was quiet, she was allowed back into the room. Gradually Julie's window banging behaviour died out, particular because her mother made sure that Julie got lots of praise and attention for good behaviour, like helping with the housework, playing quietly and so on.

Eric used to hit other residents. The staff had to stop Eric to protect the others. They often told him off for his bad behaviour. Eric's hitting behaviour was maintained by staff attention.

The staff decided to use Time-Out. Every time Eric hit someone the staff said "Stop that". They took care not to say anything else whilst they excluded him. He was allowed back into the room when quiet. Gradually, Eric hit people less. Of course, the staff made sure that Eric was able to earn regular attention for appropriate behaviour.

Note that Time-Out is used only with severe misbehaviour. It is always used with a verbal warning, like "No", so that this will be a "green light" for good behaviour and will eventually control behaviour on its own.

For Time-*Out* to work there must be Time-*In*. In other words reinforcement must be regularly available for appropriate behaviour. Otherwise, even taking someone directly to the Time-Out area is more reinforcing than doing nothing all day.

You must always make sure that removal from the situation is not reinforcing. For example, removing Peggy from the group for biting her hands would not work if Peggy did not like being in the group. You would be reinforcing her for hand biting.

REPAIRING THE DAMAGE

Another technique to make sure problem behaviour is not reinforced is to make the person repair any damage he/she has done. This also teaches the person good behaviour at the same time.

Example:

Gareth does not like doing puzzles. It is reinforcing for him to get out of doing puzzles by throwing pieces on the floor. The teacher has decided that *every time* Gareth does this he will be required to pick up all the pieces and finish the puzzle.

The teacher is making sure that throwing toys on the floor is *NEVER* reinforced. He is also making sure that Gareth is learning how to do puzzles.

Repairing the damage is a way of teaching good behaviour

Lorna walks straight in from school without wiping her feet, throws her raincoat on the floor and sits down to watch T.V. Watching T.V. is an activity which Lorna finds very reinforcing, hence her bad behaviour is being reinforced.

Lorna's mother make sure that every time Lorna rushes into the house and dumps her coat on the floor she is sent straight outside with her coat and required to enter properly (wiping her feet and hanging up her coat) before she can watch T.V.

75

In this way, Lorna's mother has made sure that bad behaviour is never reinforced. She is also teaching Lorna good behaviour — wiping her feet and hanging up her coat.

SUMMARY

1. There are several ways to make sure problem behaviour is never reinforced.
2. Some of the techniques you can use are: ignoring the behaviour; Time-Out; repairing the damage.
3. The technique you use depends on what sort of reinforcers are keeping the problem behaviour going.
4. Time-Out should only be used with severe misbehaviour.

QUIZ 14

Some methods of extinction

Please tick only one answer for each question.

1. Which of the following is one way of extinguishing behaviour that is reinforced by attention:
    (a) Saying, "You can play up all you like because I'm ignoring you"
    (b) Telling off the person
    (c) Ignoring bad behaviour all the time
    (d) Ignoring bad behaviour most of the time

2. Time-Out from reinforcement is:
    (a) A form of punishment
    (b) An activity reinforcer
    (c) A special type of reinforcer
    (d) A form of extinction

3. In Time-Out the person is excluded for:
    (a) Three minutes
    (b) Half an hour
    (c) At least 3 minutes and until quiet for 20 seconds
    (d) Until quiet for 20 seconds

4. Time-Out only works if the person can get reinforcers for good behaviour. True or False

Chapter 15

Rules for coping with problem behaviour

1. Make sure the person can earn reinforcement for good behaviour. If necessary shape up good behaviour gradually.

Always make sure the person can earn reinforcement for good behaviour

2. Study what happens immediately after the person misbehaves. See what reinforcer is maintaining the problem behaviour.

3. Select a technique which makes sure the problem behaviour is *never* reinforced.

4. If you use "Time-Out" observe these rules:
    (a) Make sure it's *safe*.
    (b) Only use it for *3 minutes* or so.
    (c) Allow the person back *ONLY* when behaving properly.
    (d) Give Time-Out *IMMEDIATELY AND EVERY TIME* the problem behaviour occurs.

QUIZ 15

1. Howard regularly starts throwing his crayons about when the children in his class are doing drawing. His teacher usually sends him out of the class for the rest of the lesson. Howard's not very good at drawing and says he doesn't like it.

    How would you suggest Howard's teacher should deal with this problem?

2. Janice throws her crayons around during drawing lessons. She usually does this when her teacher is busy with other children. Janice's teacher usually stops talking to these pupils and goes over to try and stop the misbehaviour. Usually he reasons with her but, occasionally, loses his temper and shouts at her.

    Janice spends a lot of her time "hanging around" the staff, acting the fool and so on, but most of the time the staff don't have much time for her.

    How would you advise the teacher to deal with the crayon throwing **behaviour**?

3. Nick swears almost continuously. He is usually told off when he does this but sometimes people show amusement. How would you deal with this behaviour?

4. Glenn steals food from other patient's plates. How would you deal with this behaviour?

Section V

APPENDICES

Appendix A

Group work

Many people who work with the retarded do so in the group situation: —
teachers teach groups of pupils
nurses teach groups of patients
training centre staff teach groups of trainees, and so on.

Throughout this book you will have read examples of behavioural principles being applied in the group situation. It will be clear that in the group situation the same basic teaching rules apply, for example:
1. You always reinforce appropriate behaviour.
2. You never reinforce inappropriate behaviour.

ORGANISING GROUPS

There is a number of ways in which you can make group teaching more effective.

Example:

If you have ten patients and two staff available, it is often *NOT* a good idea to have two groups of five patients.

Usually, it is much better for one member of staff to involve nine patients in group activities. At the same time, the other member of staff takes patients out of the group, one at a time, for individual teaching. These individual sessions need only be, say, 5 to 10 minutes long.

The system of running groups so that patients can be taken out for brief individual training sessions has the following advantages: —
1. All patients get intensive training sessions at some time during the day.
2. All patients can have individual training programmes specially devised to meet their needs.
3. If, as often happens, a member of staff is transferred, ill or involved in other work, the system does not collapse. You can continue to run the group without the individual sessions.
4. Staff experiences can be more varied and interesting. They can carry out both group and individual training.

CHOOSING REINFORCERS

Reinforcers differ from individual to individual. Hence, care must be taken to provide a variety of reinforcers so that these individual preferences can be taken into account.

Another approach is to use a *TOKEN SYSTEM*. A token system is simply when token reinforcers are given for appropriate behaviour. These tokens can be exchanged later for other reinforcers.

Anything can be used as a token — plastic counters, ticks in a book, gold stars on a chart, and so on.

The person should be able to "buy" a wide range of reinforcers with his tokens. (Do not, of course, deprive the person of his basic rights to food, warmth, bedding, medical care and so on. Tokens should be used to buy *EXTRA* privileges).

Tokens can be used to buy an enormous variety of reinforcers. Below is a list of just *some* of the things tokens have been used to buy, hire or play:

Sweets	Cinema visits
Cigarettes	Chats with doctor
Toiletries	Watching T.V.
Games	Record player and records
Puzzles	Toys
Books	Pop
Comics	Fruit
Pens	Watches
Pencils	Radio
Paper	Pinball machine
Flowers	**One arm bandit**

The value of tokens must be learned. Obviously, people do not automatically know that tokens will enable them to buy other reinforcers.

One way to teach the value of tokens is to give the person tokens and let him exchange them immediately for other reinforcers. When you are sure he has learned to value the tokens, you can require him to keep them for gradually longer periods of time until he only exchanges them for other reinforcers at certain times during the day.

Token systems can be used with individuals or groups.

Examples:

Johnny doesn't like school and rarely finishes his work. His teacher tells him that she is going to give him a token for every work assignment he completes. At the end of the day he can swop his tokens for sweets, comics or small toys. He can also save up his tokens, if he likes, for a trip to the zoo.

On Ward A, there are six patients who cannot dress themselves. A teaching programme is worked out and an hour a day is set aside. During this time the patients are taught and, if they succeed at the step they are learning, they receive a token. At the end of the hour they can exchange their tokens for sweets, drinks, cigarettes, magazines, and so on.

On Ward B, the staff decide that they will institute a token system for all the patients all day to try and encourage as much positive behaviour as they can. They made a list of the behaviour they wanted to encourage: —
Getting to places on time (e.g., meals, workshops)
Keeping themselves clean and tidy
Helping with domestic tasks
Making their own beds
Talking sensibly with other patients
Eating neatly

Every time individual patients show good behaviour in any of these areas they are given a token. Twice a week, they are able to exchange their tokens for a wide range of other reinforcers.

CHOOSING GROUP ACTIVITIES

Group activities must be carefully selected to match the abilities of the group members. If your group members have very varied abilities you may have to select different activities for different people.

The *Developmental Checklist* should help you find out what members of your group can do, and choose activities that are appropriate.

We want to gradually build up what the group members can do, so don't choose activities that are too easy or too hard. It is also important to choose group activities which are varied. There would not be much point in spending the whole week just doing pencil and paper exercises.

Select a variety of activities, so that all the important areas of development are covered. The *Developmental Checklist* should give you an idea of what areas are important.

CHOOSING INDIVIDUAL ACTIVITIES

We have already seen that it is often best to organise groups so that each group member can have some individual training during the day.

The *Developmental Checklist* should help you choose individual training activities. Individual sessions should be used to teach things that the person finds difficult to learn in the group situation (e.g. eye contact, toileting, dressing, feeding, washing, etc.).

Individual sessions can also be used to *create* a group. Patients who are not very capable can be taught the skills that they must have to be able to work in a group (e.g. sitting down, concentration, obeying simple instructions, etc.).

ORGANISING STAFF

It is best *NOT* to put staff in charge of groups of *patients*. It is best to put staff in charge of *activities*.

One staff member can be in charge of running a group of patients, whilst another staff member takes individuals out of the group for individual training.

Example:

If two members of staff are teaching a group of ten residents self help skills, group activities can be carried out in the dormitory with one staff member, whilst the other member of staff takes individual residents into the bowl room to teach them washing, toothbrushing and shaving.

The same approach could be used to toilet train ward residents, teach a new job in an A.T.C., help schoolchildren with their individual learn-problems and in many other teaching situations.

TIMETABLING

Obviously, staff must know what they are meant to be doing at any time during the day.

Drawing up a timetable which lists group activities and also lists which members of staff should be doing what, is obviously helpful.

It is particularly important in situations where staff change regularly.

A good timetable covers all the activities that go on throughout the day. It should name the members of staff who are responsible for these activities.

SUMMARY

1. Organise your groups so that you can take individuals out of the group for teaching.

2. Choose reinforcers suitable for the whole group. One way to do this is to set up a token system.

3. Select group activities which match the abilities of the group members.

4. Make staff responsible for *activities* not groups of people.

5. Timetable your activities, so everyone knows what is meant to be going on.

6. Remember, *the basic rules of learning still apply.* Reinforce appropriate behaviour and never reinforce inappropriate behaviour. Use shaping and chaining where necessary.

Appendix B

Principles in action

This book has dealt with the basic principles of *deciding what to teach,* and *how to teach* retarded people.

The best way to work out a teaching programme is as follows:—
1. Observe and record.
2. Decide teaching targets.
3. Identify reinforcers.
4. Keep baseline records.
5. Select teaching method.
6. Check progress and revise programme.

The examples that follow show, in outline, how the approach is used in the practical situation.

A

David was five years old and, although he had no behaviour problems, his learning had been slow and his mother was concerned that he could not dress or undress himself. She reported that she had tried but he "never got the hang of it".

Observation and recording

The *Developmental Checklist* showed that David's development was fairly even — with one or two gaps — but that his *Self-Help skills* were particularly poor; he was at Level 12 in dressing.

Deciding what to teach

Mum's priority was for David to learn to dress and undress himself. As there were five other children in the family, it was agreed to start by teaching David undressing at bedtime.

Identifying reinforcers

David responded well to praise and also showed pleasure whenever he succeeded in a new task.

Baseline records

For one week Mum noted how much David could do by himself; he could kick off his shoes and, some nights, managed his socks.

Teaching methods

Backward chaining used in conjunction with physical, gestural, and verbal prompts (see Chapters 5 and 6) seemed the most effective method of teaching David to undress and a step-by-step programme was worked out.

Checking progress

Because of other family commitments, Mum did not keep accurate records of progress, but she reported that after three months David could undress, if helped with buttons, and that he was also learning to put on his pyjamas. She felt that some of the other gaps in David's skills would have to wait till he got to school.

Comment

David had the necessary skills to undress but had been unable to learn the task because the chain was too long. Although his mother was very busy with five other children in the family, and she was unable to keep good records, she did use the correct teaching procedure, and the programme helped David learn.

B

Stephen was a four-year-old boy referred to a special unit because of his difficult behaviour. He was said to spend a lot of time running about; he would not sit down or play constructively. He would never do what he was told (in fact he often did the opposite) and he did not mix with others.

Observation and recording

Stephen was observed using the *Developmental Checklist*. His skills were generally at level 18. However, he did not have two of the basic co-operation skills. He did not sit down at a table without a fuss and did not co-operate.

Deciding what to teach

It was decided to teach Stephen to sit down and play constructively for increased periods of time and also to obey simple commands without fuss.

Identifying reinforcers

Stephen's main reinforcer was running around. Given the opportunity to choose from a variety of activities, he consistently chose to run around the room. It was decided to use this activity as a reinforcer. We also, of course, used lots of social reinforcements as well.

Baseline records

Stephen was told to "Come here" and "Put on your coat" four times each. He did not obey either of these commands. Every time Stephen sat down he was timed. It was found that he never sat down for more than 2 or 3 seconds, when required to.

Teaching methods

It was decided to shape up Stephen's sitting behaviour by expecting him to sit and play for longer periods (initially five seconds) with physical prompts if necessary, before letting him run around. We tried to make this more likely by giving him tasks at the right level to do.

Whenever Stephen obeyed a command he was praised and given the chance to move around. If he did not obey commands the first time he was not asked again, but was physically prompted.

Checking progress

Stephen progressed very quickly. Within two weeks he was sitting quietly at a table playing constructively for more than five minutes. He also came when called and put on his coat nine times out of ten. It was decided to extend the time he would sit and play and teach him to co-operate on more difficult tasks.

Comments

Many retarded children are described as over-active and Stephen, although he showed satisfactory skills in many areas, had never been taught to sit still and work at a task. The key to the success of the programme lay in breaking the task into very small steps, and using a strong reinforcer.

C

Freda was 40 years old and had spent the last 20 years in hospital. She did not do much that was constructive around the ward but had an unpleasant habit of coming up to people and chewing her hands in front of them, whilst making peculiar noises.

Observation and recording

On the *Developmental Checklist*, the staff were surprised to find that, although Freda did not do much round the ward, her skills were generally at Level 19. She was also able to do some of the items on the *Advanced Developmental Checklist* (Appendix C).

The staff observed Freda's hand-chewing behaviour over several days. They found that she only chewed when there was a member of staff near her and that the member of staff usually said something to her, such as "Stop that Freda, you hands won't look pretty if you do that".

Deciding what to teach

It was decided that because Freda had so many useful skills, she should be given more opportunity to use them, so that eventually she would be able to go to the workshops. It was also decided to extinguish her hand-chewing behaviour.

Identifying reinforcers
Freda's main reinforcer was staff attention.

Baseline records
The staff counted over three days how many times Freda chewed her hands. She did it on average 30 times a day. They also timed how long she helped round the ward or occupied herself constructively with toys, T.V., etc. She did this for about 10 minutes a day on average.

Teaching method
Freda was expected to help on the ward several times a day, e.g. laying the tables. She was praised warmly for her efforts. Other activities, e.g. toys and books, were always available to her and she was prompted to use these and praised when she did so.

As her hand chewing could not cause her much harm it was ignored; the staff walked away when she started chewing. A notice was put on the ward door to this effect so that visitors would not intermittently reinforce her by commenting.

Checking progress
At first, Freda's hand chewing got worse (50 times a day) but, after two weeks, it had dropped to zero. Working round the ward and playing constructively became reinforcing for her because of the praise she was given. Within a month she was occupying herself constructively 50 per cent of her time.

Comments
Often in large group situations where staff are few in number, people learn unacceptable ways of getting attention. With Freda, increasing constructive activities and paying more attention to "sensible" behaviour helped extinguish her hand chewing.

D

Jenny was 17 and attended an adult training centre. She didn't do very much there, except industrial work. Jenny didn't do anything useful at home. Her Mum had been wrongly told by "experts" when Jenny was small that "she'll never learn anything". She decided, with us, to start a teaching programme.

Observation and recording
When Mum completed the *Checklist* she found Jenny had learned more than she thought, but there were many gaps in her skills.

Deciding what to teach

Two targets were selected to begin the programme. These were things that the family thought most important, and which the observations showed could be taught to Jenny. They were:
1. Undressing at bedtime.
2. Occupying herself usefully at home.

Identifying reinforcers

Jenny liked to hear music on T.V. or the radio and also found adult attention and praise reinforcing.

Baseline records

Target 1. Records showed that Jenny *could* undress herself but, on average, did this only two nights out of seven. On other nights she made such a fuss that someone would do this for her to get peace.

Target 2. Jenny sometimes sat in front of T.V., or flicked through books. She never did either of these things for more than seven minutes, then started annoying adults, stopping only briefly when told to be quiet. Records showed that Jenny got lots of attention for being annoying but, when she was quiet, it was such a relief for everyone that she was left alone.

Teaching method

Target 1. Mum decided to reinforce undressing at bedtime by giving Jenny praise and letting her have music on her radio *immediately* she undressed. She did not get to hear the radio if she needed assistance.

Target 2. Mum agreed to pay attention to Jenny for being quiet and for doing any useful activity.

Checking progress

Records were kept of how often Jenny undressed properly at bedtime, and the length of time Jenny spent playing quietly after coming home from the adult training centre.

Jenny learned to undress herself *every* night by the end of the second week of the programme. Time spent doing useful things after getting home went up from seven minutes an evening to 20 minutes an evening.

The programme was then revised to teach Jenny more skills to occupy herself in the evening.

Comments

Like many handicapped people Jenny could do more things than she did regularly. Although backward chaining is usually used to teach dressing/undressing, straightforward reinforcement was used here because Jenny *could* undress, but did not do so regularly. Each person's problems have to be looked at individually — there is no "cook-book answer".

E

Anna was seven years old and she was making steady progress at school except that she apparently couldn't learn colours.

Observation and recording

Anna could do all items up to Level 18, except she was only at Level 16 in colours.

Deciding what to teach

Anna was progressing well generally, so it was decided to set aside individual sessions during each day to teach her colour skills.

Identifying reinforcers

Anna worked well in class for praise from her teacher but had learned to dislike colour matching and naming because she failed so often. She loved "helping teacher", so it was decided to allow her to do a daily job for the teacher after each individual session as an activity reinforcer.

Baseline records

Anna consistently failed to match colours whenever more than two were present.

Teaching method

It was decided that shaping would be effective but only if the task were broken down into very small steps. At first, Anna had to place a smooth red disc beside another identical red disc, instead of beside a smaller round black square. Her teacher gradually moved through steps until Anna was able to separate red discs from black squares of the same size and surface. Other colours were then slowly introduced. Only when Anna could match colours well did she move on to more advanced colour skills.

Checking progress

Teacher checked progress at the end of each session and began every new session by repeating the previous session's last task.

Comments

Normal children learn colour concepts at widely differing ages and it is important not to try and teach them to handicapped children unless they have the necessary other skills. It is not a good idea to select teaching colours until you have taught a child other new skills even when colours are the most obvious gap.

F

Susie was eight years old and her parents were very worried because they said she wouldn't talk to anyone except her family. She had never talked to other people since starting school.

Observation and recording

Susie talked to only seven people — all at home. Her language at home was up to other levels on the *Developmental Checklist*.

Deciding what to teach

Susie had to be taught to talk to other people, particularly at school.

Identifying reinforcers

Susie liked adult praise and attention and particularly liked painting

Baseline records

Over a two week period in school it was noted that, irrespective of praise or threats, she never talked to anyone — only nodding or shaking her head.
activities.

Teaching method

It was decided to use shaping and, on arrival at school, Susie was taken aside briefly by her teacher. She was reinforced for attempting to whisper "yes" in response to a simple question and her teacher gradually demanded more volume and words when alone with Susie. Once she was answering simple questions clearly when alone with the teacher, another adult joined the situation. This continued till language was well established in class, then more people and different situations were used.

Susie was always reinforced for answering and talking properly.

Checking progress

Records were kept showing exactly who Susie spoke to in school, where this happened, and how many other people were present. Within four weeks she learned to converse with familiar staff and children anywhere in school.

Comments

Susie was an unusual girl. Her conversation at home showed she could talk well, but did not choose to at school. If she had been unable to talk at all, a completely different approach would have been necessary.

Appendix C

Advanced Developmental Checklist

This checklist is organised on similar lines to the *Developmental Checklist* (see Chapter 8).

The items are grouped in four Sections under five developmental levels from (a) to (e). These correspond roughly to the range from five years to adolescence. Where no items are given at a particular developmental level, this means that no new skills are acquired at that stage. Simply tick what the person can do and you will be able to see from the list what he needs to learn next.

Remember to try and ensure that the person develops evenly in all the areas.

Sections

	Page
Movement and travel	94
Social skills (getting on with others)	95
Self-help	96
Washing and self care	
Dressing and care of clothes	
Eating and drinking	
Food preparation	
Shopping	
Domestic tasks	
Occupation	99
Books and writing	
Handling things	
Number, quantity and size	
Time	
Money and budgeting	

MOVEMENT AND TRAVEL

(a) Crosses street safely.
Can go short distances on foot safely, e.g. to school.
Stands and walks acceptably (does not attract attention).

(b) Can use swing doors safely.
Does not walk into other pedestrians.
Uses 'bus when supervised.
Uses 'bus alone if given precise instructions and the exact fare.

(c) Can go to several places on foot, within about a mile from home, safely.
Uses 'bus alone for familiar journey and finds own fare.

(d) Uses lifts properly.
Uses moving stairs properly.
Can make a journey involving two buses.

(e) Uses pedestrian crossing.
Enquires about and makes unfamiliar journeys.
Can use trains and timetables.
Keeps ticket for sensible period.
Follows directions such as, "Take the first turning on the right and the second on the left".

SOCIAL SKILLS (getting on with others)

(a) Plays simple table games, e.g. snap, dominoes, snakes and ladders.
Observes rules.
If loses, does not fuss.
Occupies self simply, without prompting, e.g. watches T.V., plays with toys.

(b)

(c) Does not borrow without permission.
Takes care of others' belongings.
Answers 'phone, gives sensible answers.
Asks for help when needed.

(d) Is polite, e.g. says "please" and "thank you", knocks on doors, etc.
Obeys rules, e.g. silence, "No Smoking".
Chooses T.V. programme.
Dials telephone number.

(e) Uses public telephone.
Uses directory or gets number from operator.
Plays difficult games, e.g. ping-pong, monopoly.
Understands rules and scoring.
Organises leisure time constructively, e.g. makes models or clothes, has a hobby, is a member of a club.

SELF-HELP

Washing and self-care

(a) Baths self if someone fills bath.

(b) Shampoos, rinses and dries hair properly.
Uses make-up appropriately.
Fills own bath.

(c) Can wash and put plaster on small cut.
Washes regularly without reminder.
Does not smell.
Combs and brushes hair regularly.

(d) Dials 999 in an emergency.
Takes care of nails.
Takes care of self during periods (girls).

(e) Knows what items to use for: headaches, cuts, stomach upsets, colds, etc., and where to get them from.
Contacts G.P., if necessary.
Contacts dentist, if necessary.
Gets hair cut.

Dressing and care of clothes

(a) Can clean own shoes.

(b)

(c) Hangs up clothes.
Cleans shoes regularly.
Ties bow (girls) or tie (boys).
Hangs clothes on washing line.

(d) Keeps self neat and tidy throughout the day.
Changes underwear regularly.
Wears the right clothes at the right time, e.g. **coat when raining**.
Sews on buttons.

(e) Uses launderette or washes own clothes.
Irons clothes.
Uses dry cleaners if necessary.

Eating and drinking

Manners

(a) Does not spill food.
Sits properly.
(b)
(c) Does not eat with mouth open.
Helps self to reasonable quantities of food, condiments, etc.
(d) Does not talk with mouth full.
Can eat difficult foods acceptably, e.g. soup, chicken, boiled eggs.
(e) Eats inoffensively in public.

Food preparation

(a) Makes sandwiches.
Can measure out teaspoonfuls of sugar for tea and coffee.
(b) Makes pot of tea and cup of instant coffee.
Makes toast.
Operates rings and grill correctly under supervision.
(c) Uses tin opener.
Heats up simple foods, e.g. soup, beans (may not light stove).
Peels vegetables.
(d) Uses stove without supervision.
Fries simple foods, e.g. eggs, sausages, etc.
(e) Can grill simple foods, e.g. fish fingers.
Can cook a meal, perhaps using tins.

Shopping

(a) Can make purchase from one shop when given correct money and instructions.
(b) Can go to right shops for simple items, e.g. bread, papers, apples, if given correct money.
(c) Can deal with ordinary and self-service shops if given correct money.
Can eat in self-service cafe.
(d) Can give correct money or is able to check change.
Can order meal from waitress in cafe.
Knows where to get stamps.
(e) Buys small items of clothing — chooses sensibly.
Buys all own clothes — chooses sensibly.
Knows where to get application forms.

Domestic tasks

(a) Clears table.
    Dusts furniture.
    Sweeps floor.

(b) Washes floor adequately.
    Dries up and puts things away.

(c) Tidies a room.
    Keeps own room or dormitory area clean.

(d) Makes own bed.
    Lays table.
    Uses vacuum cleaner.
    Is routinely responsible for some task, e.g. tidying the living room.

(e) Cleans windows.
    Does remunerative part-time work, e.g. newspaper round.
    Has a full-time job.

OCCUPATION
Books and writing
(a) Recognises own name.
Prints simple words without copying (spelling may not be correct).
(b) Reads price labels.
Occupies self with magazine and picture books.
Writes at least 12 words without copying (no spelling mistakes).
(c) Recognises at least 50 words.
Can read easy instructions.
Reads children's books.
Writes occasional letter, may need help with address.
(d) Reads simple newspaper, e.g. Mirror.
(e) Reads simple novels.
Fills in simple application form.
Writes proper letters containing news and useful information.

Handling things
(a)
(b) Uses glue and sellotape neatly.
(c) Cuts pictures out accurately.
Can use: hammer, saw, screwdriver, spade, rake, etc.
Can tie adequate knots.
(d)
(e)

Number, quantity and size
(a) Counts at least 20 objects.
Can do simple sums involving numbers up to 10.
(b) Tells or shows you difference between high/low, above/below, on/off.
Counts at least 50 objects.
Knows number sequence without having to count (e.g. knows 4 comes after 3).
When asked can give you: heavy or light, full or empty, big, medium or small, from objects.
(c) Counts to 100 in tens.
Measures weight with simple scales.

(d)

(e) Can tell or show you what: pair, couple, dozen, ½-dozen, is.
Measures with ruler.
Knows what half and one quarter means, e.g. is able to divide an object or objects into half or quarter when asked.

Time

(a) Tells you what day tomorrow will be and what day yesterday was.

(b) Tells time to nearest quarter hour.

(c) Tells time to the minute.
Responds to time by going to lunch, switching on T.V., etc.

(d) Can set alarm clock.
Understands time intervals, e.g. knows that 2.00 to 4.30 is 2½ hours.

(e)

Money and budgeting

(a) Knows whether one coin is worth more or less than another.

(b) Recognises all coins.
Knows some everyday prices, e.g. sweets, cigarettes.

(c) Adds various coins, up to 10p.
Knows how much change he would get from 10p.

(d) Adds various coins, up to £1.
Knows how much change he should get from 50p.
Puts some money aside for later (does not spend all money at once).

(e) Is able to work out simple expenses sums, e.g. 'bus fare, plus cigarettes.
Saves with a bank or Post Office.
Can read prices and give correct money.
Can fill in postal order correctly.

Section VI

ANSWERS TO QUIZZES

ANSWERS

QUIZ 1
1. (b)
2. (c)
3. (b), (c), (d), (f), (h)
4. (c)
5. Ted hits, bites, scratches, kicks, other patients. (Any answer describing what Ted *does* is acceptable).
6. True.
7. False.
8. False.

QUIZ 2
1. (b)
2. (c)
3. (c)
4. (a)
5. (d)

Types of reinforcer
1. Anything that strengthens your behaviour is a reinforcer for you.
2. a) F b) T c) A d) S e) T f) S g) F h) A i) F j) S k) A
3. For example: hugs, kisses.
4. .. .. fish and chips, glass of squash.
5. .. .. cigarette coupons, family allowance books.
6. . .. a game of football, a trip to the park.

But remember these reinforcers are not necessarily reinforcers for everyone or for anyone all the time and lots of things can be reinforcers.

QUIZ 3
1. (d)
2. (a) The bathroom
   (b) Getting away from having a bath.
3. (a) The time (6 o'clock.)
   (b) Sweets.
4. A green light means you will receive a reinforcer if you behave in a certain way.
5. A red light means you will not receive a reinforcer if you behave in a certain way.
6. a) The sight of the toilet.
      Sitting on the toilet.
      Time of day.
      Bladder pressure.
   b) Time of day.
      The lights turned on.
      Someone telling you to get up.
      The sight of the clothes.
   c) Cake shop in shop hours or feeling hungry.
   d) Sight of the T.V.
      Time of day.

QUIZ 4
1. False
2. False
3. (d)
4. (b)
5. (c)
6. Food and drink — Give him a selection and see what he chooses.
   Activity — Give him a selection of toys, etc., and see what he chooses.
   Play games with him and see what he prefers to play.
   Watch him and see what he chooses to do in his own time.
   Social — Always use social reinforcers. See if he responds to specific ones, e.g. hugs or praise.
   Token — Does he respond to common tokens, e.g. money, stars? If not, is it worthwhile teaching their value? (See Appendix A)

Using reinforcers
1. (b)   2. (c)   3. (d)   4. (d)
5. (b)   6. True   7. False   8. True

QUIZ 5

1. (b)
2. Verbal, gestural, physical.
3. (d)
4. (b)
5. (b)
6. One way you could teach Pete would be to say "Pete, push the car", take his hand, and guide him through the motions of pushing the car. Every time he does this, immediately reinforce him with praise and, if necessary, another reinforcer which you have chosen for him. Gradually you would withdraw this physical prompt. Perhaps you would move your hand gradually up his arm to his elbow, then to the top of his arm and then remove it altogether.

7. One way you could teach Jock would be to make the task very easy to start with and gradually build up his skills. You could start with large beads with large holes and teach Jock to thread them onto, say, drinking straws. When he had learned this you could teach him to thread smaller beads onto fairly stiff string or flex. You could then use even smaller beads and finer string until he was able to thread very small beads onto cotton.
You would of course reinforce Jock *immediately* and *every time* he threaded a bead. You may have to use prompts to guide Jock through the motions of threading, but you would gradually fade these out.
8. You would want to build up sitting-down behaviour gradually. You could start by reinforcing the patients for sitting down for a few seconds. You could then gradually extend the length of time they had to sit down to earn a reinforcer until they would sit down for 5 or 10 minutes at a time.

QUIZ 6

1. (a)
2. (d)
3. (c)
4. (a), (d), (c), (b)
5. (b)
6. (b)

7. You would probably decide to break down this task into small steps, for example:
   1) Puts one piece on table
   2) Puts second piece onto first piece
   3) Puts third piece onto 2nd piece
   4) Puts fourth piece onto 3rd piece
   5) Puts fifth piece onto 4th piece.
First you would probably show Louise how to put it all together.
You would then present her with the jigsaw with only one piece missing. You would say "Put it in" and, if necessary, guide her hand. You would repeat this step until Louise could put the piece in without a prompt.
You would then present Louise with the jigsaw with two pieces missing and teach her to put both pieces in. When she had learned this you would give her the jigsaw with three pieces missing, and so on, until she could do the whole jigsaw on her own.
You would, of course, reinforce Louise with praise and if necessary, another reinforcer, *immediately* and *every time* that she put the last piece in.

103

QUIZ 7

1. (d)
2. (c)
3. (b)
4. (a)

QUIZ 8

1. (c)
2. (a) Sits down at a table without fuss
   (b) Looks at you when you call his name
   (c) Looks at the objects he is working with
   (d) Co-operates
3. (b)
4. (d)

QUIZ 9

1. (c)
2. (a) O
   (b) L
   (c) O
3. (d) L
   (e) O
   (f) O
   (g) L

QUIZ 10

1. (d)
2. (b)
3. (d)
4. (a)
5. (c)
6. Gerald will probably go quiet when given food. This will reinforce his mother for giving him food when he screams. Giving Gerald food will reinforce his screaming. Hence Gerald will be more likely to scream at teatime and his mother will be more likely to feed him when he screams. The "green light" is teatime.
7. You would probably want to record.
   a) For how long he bites his fingers.
   b) What happens before he does it.
   c) What happens after he does it.
   You would use a chart headed: DATE, TIME, WHAT HAPPENED BEFORE? HOW LONG DID HE BITE HIS FINGERS?, WHAT HAPPENED AFTER?

QUIZ 11

1. (c)
2. False
3. True
4. True
5. True
6. False

QUIZ 12

1. (c)
2. (b)
3. You should make sure Gerry can earn lots of reinforcers for good behaviour. Provide lots of suitable toys and equipment and, whenever he is playing appropriately, reinforce him.
   The reinforcers you use would obviously depend on the individual, but you should be able to gradually shape up appropriate play behaviour.

QUIZ 13
1. (a)
2. (d)
3. (c)
4. False

QUIZ 14
1. (c)
2. (d)
3. (c)
4. True

QUIZ 15
1. Howard's crayon-throwing behaviour is being reinforced by getting out of drawing. (He doesn't like drawing). His teacher should reinforce Howard whenever he draws and may shape up his drawing skills by starting with easy materials and gradually building on this. Howard should also be made to pick up the crayons when he has thrown them.

2. Janice's crayon throwing behaviour is being reinforced by staff attention. (She spends a lot of time trying to get attention from the staff). Her teacher should make sure Janice gets lots of attention when she is working properly.

   She should never pay attention when Janice throws the crayons around. If it is not possible to ignore this behaviour, Janice should be given Time-Out for about three minutes (until quiet for 20 seconds or so) and then allowed to return to the class, picking up her crayons on the way.

   (Notice that getting Janice to pick up her crayons, which involves attention, is done several minutes after the bad behaviour so that crayon throwing is not reinforced).

3. Nick's continuous swearing is being maintained by the attention it earns him. It should be ignored completely. Everyone Nick comes into contact with must ignore Nick everytime he swears. He should receive lots of fuss and attention when he talks sensibly without swearing.

4. Glenn's behaviour is probably being maintained by the food he gets from others' plates. He should be made to repair the damage (give the food, or an equivalent amount, back). He may also undergo a Time-Out procedure. You could immediately remove his food for three minutes or so following his food stealing to make sure he doesn't eat (i.e., reinforce himself) immediately after stealing food.